# AN INTRODUCTION TO
# EVOLUTIONARY PRODUCT DEVELOPMENT

## ARTHUR O. EGER

WITH CONTRIBUTIONS
BY HUUB EHLHARDT
& FERRY VERMEULEN

eleven
international publishing

Published, sold and distributed by
Eleven International Publishing
P.O. Box 85576
2508 CG The Hague
The Netherlands
Tel.: +31 70 33 070 33
Fax: +31 70 33 070 30
e-mail: sales@budh.nl
www.elevenpub.com

Sold and distributed in USA and Canada
International Specialized Book Services
920 NE 58th Avenue, Suite 300
Portland, OR 97213-3786, USA
Tel: 1-800-944-6190 (toll-free)
Fax: +1-503-280-8832
orders@isbs.com
www.isbs.com

Eleven International Publishing
is an imprint of Boom uitgevers Den Haag.

ISBN 978-94-6236-058-7

Design & Layout: Rob Hulsbosch · www.hulsbosch.net
Printed in The Netherlands

'If you want to know where the rainbow ends
It's you who've got to go there and find it my friend'

*Adios Lounge – Thelonious Monster featuring Tom Waits*

# CONTENTS

# 1 INTRODUCTION

## 1.1 Preface

For any organization it is important to maintain or strengthen its
market share by keeping its products and/or services up to date.
Industrial designers often take part in the team that develops new
products. Sometimes they even lead such teams. They can use a number
of methods and techniques that are helpful for some of their tasks, but
for others (especially for form giving) designers still need qualities such
as experience and intuition. This book will show that this seemingly
intuitive way of working has regularities and patterns that can be
reproduced. These will lead to a theory that can help a designer with the
short-term future development of products. According to this theory,
six phases can be distinguished in a product's life. These phases will be
called product phases, each of which is described by means of product
characteristics. It will be demonstrated that products generally follow
the product phases in the same order. The aim of the research described
in this book is two-sided, since it endeavors to improve our insight into
a product's life cycle and, on the other hand, to develop a means that
can help a designer in the process of product development.

## 1.2 Definitions

The terms product development, innovation, design, styling, industrial
design engineering and functionality are used with different meanings.
Some use product development only in relation to the development
of a new or improved product. For others the search that precedes the
design of the new product, the development of production methods
and the development of the market introduction are also elements of
what they call product development. The term 'design' is even used in
a wider context. While an optician may have a 'design collection' of
glasses in his shop, someone who develops software may also call his
concept a 'design'. To avoid misunderstandings about the definitions of
these terms, the definitions used in this book are presented first. Most
of the time the term 'product' means a material object that performs
a function. However, in this book a 'product' can also be a service or a
combination of a product and a service, meaning that products are not

only bicycles, shavers or mobiles, but also holidays, travelling or bank services. This results in the following definition of a product.

### Product
A (physical) result of the creative or artistic mind that is 'produced' in series or that is mass produced and offered for sale.

### Product Development
The field of dealing with the design, creation, production and marketing of new products.

### Innovation
1. The act of innovating; introduction of a new idea into the market-place in the form of a new product or service, or an improvement in organization or (production) process;
2. A change effected by innovating.

### Design
The appearance of the whole or part of an artefact, including any pattern or texture applied to its surface.

### Styling
A distinctive manner or way of form giving, e.g. a unique decoration or an expressive shape.

### Industrial Design Engineering
The design and engineering of functional objects that can be produced in series or that can be mass-produced.

### Functionality
In this study the word functionality relates to the technical performance of a product. Does the product function – in a technological way – as the user expects? According to this definition, the functionality can be good while, for instance, the comfort, safety and user-friendliness of the product are insufficient. Consequently, this functionality is sometimes referred to as technological functionality. Wherever this study refers to another kind of performance, this will be stated, for example in the case of ergonomic or economic functionality.

This thesis introduces two new concepts.

### Product Phase
A phase in the economic product life cycle of a product that has distinguishing features defined by product characteristics.

### Product Characteristic
A feature of a product phase that is characteristic of this phase. Product characteristics may concern the functionality, emotional benefits, price, market, product development, production, promotion, ethics, etc.

## 1.3 Determination of the Concept

The theory of Evolutionary Product Development originates from the design practice of Van Dijk/Eger/Associates (nowadays referred to as WeLL Design), a major Dutch design company, founded in 1979. From the very beginning, Arthur Eger – one of the founders of the company – tried to describe the experience of the bureau in terms of a model. The first publication was realized in 1987 in *Dutch Design* (Eger, 1987) on the occasion of a large exhibition that five museums in the Netherlands had organized on the subject of design in the Netherlands. This publication identified five product phases. The sixth product phase, namely awareness, was first described in an article in *NieuwsTribune* (Eger, 1993), and later in the book *Succesvolle Productontwikkeling* (Successful Product Development) (Eger, 1996).

In the theory of Evolutionary Product Development the dynamics of the role that products play in society or on the market are the starting point. These dynamics are regarded as an evolutionary process. Until the late 1980s, product development was generally considered to be a linear process. Successful new (versions of) products were considered to be the next logical step in the continuous improvement of the product with regard to the price and performance. The basic thought behind this idea was based on the – in practice non-existing – principle of perfect competition, a term derived from neoclassical economic theory. According to this theory, a product can survive in a market only if it has an improved performance/price ratio, relative to its predecessors.

In the last quarter of the previous century, this principle has received a great deal of critique. Development processes (e.g. product development) seemed to be much less predictable and unambiguous than the linear model suggested. In different fields of interest in which innovation processes are studied, such as economics and technology studies, research was initiated to find new explanatory models that focus on the complicated way in which innovation progresses. It is striking that this research, which is based on very different points of view owing to the many research backgrounds, ended with the same type of explanations, namely evolutionary models. Several authors – such as Steadman (1979), Petroski (1992) and Norman (1988, 1992) – engaged in the field of product development suggested an evolutionary process, although the practical consequences of this point of view remained unnoticed for many years. The linear model remained the generally accepted theory in studies of product development and innovation management, as can be seen, for instance, in the approach followed in almost all introductory texts on design methodology. Despite this, those practical implications are far-reaching. A number of economic phenomena, such as partial path dependency, embeddedness and technological lock-in, cannot be explained by the linear model and are therefore traditionally considered anomalies. However, they can be explained when an Evolutionary Product Development model is used as a framework. This is an important reason for continuing to investigate the possibilities of an evolutionary vision on product development and innovation.

### 1.3.1 Product Phases

The model states that each of six product phases displays a typical pattern of product characteristics. Every company making money through the development, production or marketing of products will have to deal with this phenomenon. Managing it requires skills with respect to both management of product development and design methodology, as well as a sound awareness of design history.
In practice, products in each phase can be found on the market, and specific knowledge is required for every phase.

FIGURE 1.3.1
The six product phases, version of 2007.

Generally speaking, the emphasis in the first phase – performance – is on new technologies. New product functions are developed, for which the functional performance of the products is the main challenge at this point. In the second phase – optimization – other knowledge is required. The market no longer accepts imperfections, and other disciplines become important. Manufacturing technology and quality control become increasingly relevant. Product development is aimed at improving performance, reliability, ergonomics and safety. In this phase, and in the following one, involving clients in the product development process is beneficial for both the product performance and the financial results of the company (Candi et al., 2010). In the third phase – itemization – high quality and safety no longer suffice. Ergonomics and styling become important success factors. Research in the field of man-machine interfaces starts playing a role. The aim of product development is to develop extra features and accessories, including special editions of the product for different trade channels and target groups (segmentation).

According to the research presented in this book, the last three phases coexist (Figure 1.3.2). Product development is aimed either at target groups that become increasingly smaller (extended segmentation) or at mass customization or co-creation, by which the customer is able to influence the final result (individualization). The ethical behaviour of the company or organization behind the product is also becoming more and more important to the customer (awareness).

FIGURE 1.3.2
The six product phases, latest version. The last three product phases occur simultaneously.

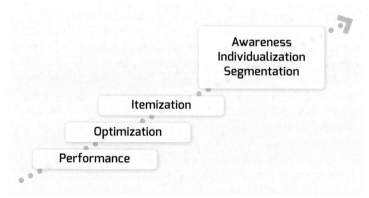

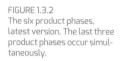

# 2 THEORIES RELATED TO INDUSTRIAL DESIGN ENGINEERING: A SHORT HISTORY

This chapter presents an overview of theories that were developed to help designers with the design and styling of products. These theories have been grouped according to themes that are based on the point of view of the researchers of the theory. Four themes can be distinguished, namely Demographic Models, Measuring Instruments, Behaviouristic Explanations and Hierarchical Structures. Besides that, some research was found that is interesting enough to mention, but that does not fit in with one of the themes. These are grouped in the section entitled, 'Other Relevant Research'. The aim of the research was to find out to what extent these theories can contribute to the defining and understanding of the product phases and to the formulation of the product characteristics that best describe the product phases.

Because history is important for the model of product phases, recent studies were considered in addition to some older ones. The publications are described in a chronological order within their theme. The conclusions drawn from the presented theories partially overlap. Some research directions, like the 'numeric aesthetics' of Bense (1954), have been abandoned because they seemed to lead to a dead end. They have still been included in this chapter because they give an impression of ideas and research of the past and also because they make this chapter more complete.

## 2.1 Demographic Models

Demographics is the science that studies quantitative aspects of the country's populations, such as age, gender, nationality, ethnicity, profession, race, mobility, home ownership, and employment status. Marketers and sociologists have tried many times to create groups based on demographics, social classes or lifestyles. The following definitions are used. Social classes are based – in a modern society – on income, influence (power) and prestige. Groups can be based on, amongst other things, region (Irish, Scottish, Welsh), religion, or age (senior citizens).

Grouping in lifestyles is based on values and the openness for change. By using signs, such as clothing, behaviour and jewellery, people can indicate to what group, class or lifestyle they (want to) belong. Products not only perform a function, they also give the owner emotional benefits. Consequently, products can – just as the use of language, manners, and participation in cultural activity – function as signals to indicate membership of a group.

### 2.1.1 Veblen (1899/1994): *the Theory of the Leisure Class*

One of the first researchers to describe groups based on demographic criteria was Thorstein Veblen. In 1899 the American sociologist Veblen (1899/1994) explained the behaviour of the upper class ('leisure class') as signs that they use to show their wealth. According to Veblen, members of the leisure class do not work with their hands, meaning that well cared-for hands with clean, unbroken nails are important to them. If they perform any physical activity, it has to be 'unproductive' and 'consumptive', such as sports (golf, tennis). They own country houses or estates. Therefore, their meadows are used to keep non-productive animals such as deer or race horses instead of cows or sheep. They wear clothes that make working with their hands difficult or impossible: clean, white shirts, lacquered shoes and folded trousers. Their wives wear tight skirts and high-heeled shoes. Their activities are obviously useless since they learn 'dead' languages (Greek, Latin), or study music or art history. A lot of time and attention is devoted to good manners and correct spelling and pronunciation of the language. They develop to become connoisseurs of antiques and wine because these are useless (not life-essential) products that only members of their class can afford to consume. A number of these signs are later copied by other, lower classes. A description such as 'white collar profession' speaks for itself.

### 2.1.2 Mitchell (1983): *the Nine American Lifestyles; who we Are and where we're Going*

In 1978 Arnold Mitchell introduced his VALS typology (Value and Lifestyle). He distinguished groups of consumers based on behaviour, activities, interests and values. He described four main categories and nine subcategories.

**Need-Driven**
It can be subdivided into 'Survivors' (5%) and 'Sustainers' (10%). According to Mitchell, this group consists mainly of elderly people with low incomes who often live in big cities.

**Outer-Directed**
A group whose motivation is greatly influenced by their peers. This group can be subdivided into 'Emulators' (45%), 'Pursuers' (10%) and 'Achievers' (22%). The biggest subgroup are the 'Emulators'. They have an income that is below average, and they are conventional and nostalgic (in the past everything used to be better). The 'Pursuers' have an average income, are younger and very ambitious. The 'Achievers'

have a higher income, are well educated, somewhat older (middle-aged), ambitious and like to show their success to the outside world.

### Inner-Directed

A group that is self-motivated, divided into 'I-am-me' (2%), 'Experiential' (2%) and 'Societally Conscious' (2%). These are relative small groups. Members of the 'I-am-me' group are young, have a high education and are individualistic. Many of them are students on low incomes for themselves, but who come from rich families. The 'Experiential' group is in some ways comparable to this group, but includes more women. Its members are also young, earn a good income and are looking for 'experiences'. The 'Societally Conscious' are socially aware and care about the environment. They often have a high income and are well educated, but despite that they live sober lives.

### Integrated

'Combined Outer- and Inner-Directed' or 'Integrated' (2%). The members of this group have high incomes (either because they have good jobs or live on 'old money'), are well educated, self-assured, tolerant and interested in art and culture.

A disadvantage of this model used to be that it was rather static, while in reality new groups form and the original groups change both in behaviour and numbers of people. At present the model is kept up-to-date by SBI (Strategic Business Insights) in California (USA).

## 2.1.3 Foot (1996): *Boom, Bust & Echo*

According to David Foot, two thirds of everything that will happen in the near future (5 to 10 years) can be predicted on the basis of demographic shifts. If you want to know how people aged 40 will behave in 5 years, all you have to do is study the behaviour of people aged 45 right now. If there are a lot of people aged 40, the behaviour of people who are currently 45 will become a trend. Unfortunately, the results of Foot's research with regard to the behaviour of people are spread throughout his book, and he does not use age categories. To make his theory useful for industrial design engineers, age categories have been created. The results of his research were collected and grouped according to these categories and are described below.[1]

### Children, 0–9 Years

This group does not feature in Foot's research. Children of this age do not usually decide for themselves (although this may depend on their ability to nag). In general, their parents decide (see Starters and Families).

### Adolescents, 10-19 Years

Adolescents do not have much money, but they do have a lot of time. This means that they have enough time to look for the cheapest offers and that they are willing to read complicated instructions and assemble

---

1 Note that the book was written in 1996 and that Foot is Canadian. Although some aspects were updated, not everything will be relevant in every country.

do-it-yourself products to save money. They live with their parents, attend concerts and sports events, go out a lot and download lots of music, films and games. They use public transport and think they are immortal.

### Starters, 20-29 Years

Just like adolescents, starters do not have much money, but they do have a lot of time. They study and start living on their own, mostly in the centre of a (big) city. They are not very critical about the quality of the products they buy. They look for bargains and spend time hunting them down. They buy in discount shops and assemble products themselves if that saves them money. Mostly they use public transport and they drink beer (a lot and cheap beer so that they can get drunk as cheaply as possible). They also behave as if they are immortal. Their favourite sports are football (soccer), tennis and hockey. They use decorative cosmetics (fashionable, with expressive colours), and they are followers of the latest fashion. They are on the look-out for a prospective partner. The first car that they buy is second-hand and inexpensive.

### Families, 30-39 Years

Starter families with small children usually have a bit more to spend, but they also have a lot of expenses due to their house, furnishings, car and children. (In the Netherlands the average age of women when they gave birth for the first time was 29 in 1996 and 28 in 1992). Because they spend a lot of money they often borrow (mortgage). They live in a suburb and want a house with a garden. They drink less, but more expensive, alcohol in the form of special beers or wine. They buy a new car every two years to 'keep up with the Joneses'. As they approach 40 they start earning more money, but have less time to spend it. They become more critical of the quality of the products they buy. They select skin care products (instead of decorative cosmetics) and engage in fewer sports (or they switch sports to golf). Because they have children, the vehicle they own will be a minivan, space wagon or SUV.

### Career Oriented, 40-49 Years

The people that belong to this group have a lot of money to spend. Their career is running smoothly, and their outgoings are declining. Their children start to go and live on their own, their mortgage has been nearly paid back and many of the products they have are good enough and do not need replacing. They have busy lives, regard quality as being important and have no time (nor do they want to take the time) to look for bargains. They buy leading brands and want good advice. They do not have time to read the user-manual, so they want simple products. They like convenience and are willing to spend money on getting it. Instead of buying a head of lettuce, they buy pre-packed, pre-washed, ready-to-use 'salad mix'. They shop at supermarkets with a wide range of products. They do not mind if all this costs a bit more as long as it does not take much time. They buy a smaller but more luxurious car. They pay almost no attention to fashion because they have already dislocated their ankles by wearing platform shoes in their 20s. They buy clothes that they know by experience fit their style. They buy more lingerie, also 'corrective' lingerie, because their bodies are not in as good shape as they used to be. About 80% need reading glasses. They are attracted to less contact-based sports, such as golf or walking. They go to musicals, ballet and classic concerts, rather than rock concerts and sports events. By the time they reach 45 they start having a midlife crisis about what they are going to do with the rest of their lives. They start their own companies or set out on a new career. They are sometimes willing to make do with a lower salary.

**Young Seniors, 50-59 Years**
Young seniors have both time and money. Their children have left home and they want good quality and service. They have enough experience with products of poor quality to have become very critical and aware of good quality. They think they have everything they need as regards products. They therefore prefer to spend their money on holidays, going out for dinner, concerts or the theatre. They prefer faraway, exclusive destinations. With regard to clothing they know what fits and suits them and are willing to pay the asking price. They are keen to be given good financial advice about how to invest their money (private banking). They are aware of their mortality (often one or both of their parents have died) and are worried about and pay attention to their state of health. They use vitamins and preventive medicines. Men encounter prostate problems, women are in, or are approaching, menopause. They spend more money on games of chance such as casino games, the lottery and bingo. They prefer quiet shops with dedicated and patient staff, and have no desire to negotiate on prices. They prefer luxurious sedans and drive them for five years or more. They often get involved in voluntary work and spend more money than others on charity. They visit museums, start collecting things (or pick up where they left off with an old collection), start a hobby, or start to read (again) in their spare time.

**Seniors, 60+**
Seniors are – to a great extent – comparable to young seniors. Many of them are retired, and because most of them have taken good care of themselves, they get a lot of money to spend and a lot of time to spend it.[2] They do not plan to save this money for their children. They are assertive and critical and want to enjoy the rest of their lives, as well as giving meaning (fulfilment) to it. However, they start to suffer more and more health problems, and their need for medication slowly increases as their mobility slowly decreases.

## What Can Be Predicted and what Cannot?
Foot claims that the near future of two-thirds of 'everything' can be predicted with the aid of demographic knowledge, at least if the behaviour is related to age. According to Foot, that is almost always the case. However, some things cannot be predicted. A surprising example is the result of elections. One would expect an aging population to vote more conservatively. However, this is untrue. Indeed, there is no relationship between age and voting behaviour. Therefore, a change in

---

2   This may differ according to country. In Europe this is the case in many countries.

the age structure of the population has no predictive value. Another example is the introduction of new products (innovations) and their direct consequences, such as the computer (and the predicted paperless office that still has not become a reality), or the discovery that smoking causes cancer, which has led very slowly to a reduction in the number of smokers. After a number of years, when the influence of the new product has become clearer, the consequences will also have become more and more predictable.

## Exclusive?

A critical note that has to be made with regard to Foot's model is that he seems to concentrate his research on people with both a higher education and a higher income. He states, for instance, that members of the 'career oriented' and 'young seniors' groups have a lot of money to spend. However, after examining the VALS typology (Section 2.1.2), Mitchell (1983) concluded that 60% of people can be regarded as belonging to a low-income category. No significant change can be expected in the situation between 1983 and 1996, although the situation improved considerably as regards Mentality (Section 2.1.4). Therefore it is questionable if Foot's theory is representative of the whole population or only of an elite group.

### 2.1.4    Motivaction Research & Strategy (2011): *Mentality*

The Mentality Model is comparable to the VALS typology, but was introduced more recently, in 1995. It was first introduced under the name 'Socioconsult'. This model is based on both opinion polls and one-to-one interviews. Apart from acquiring demographic information, emphasis is placed on the interviewees' standards and values. This type of longitudinal information gathering can be used to measure changes within and between market segments. However, these changes are small and very gradual, being 1% or 2% per annum at the most. The following segments have been distinguished within Motivaction (see Figure 2.1.1 for an overview of the results):

**Traditional Citizenry, 16%**
Moralistic, law-abiding and status quo-oriented citizens who hang on to traditions and material possessions.
*Keywords: the family as the cornerstone of society; quiet and harmonious lifestyle; solidarity with minorities and concern about the environment; acceptance of authority and rules; risk avoidance; sober and thrifty; geared towards passive entertainment; family as the central point; traditional division of roles; more women than men; few young people; fewer highly educated people.*

**Modern Citizenry, 22%**
Conformist, status-conscious citizens who look for a balance between traditional versus modern values such as consumption and enjoyment.
*Keywords: the family as the cornerstone of society; acquisition of status and respect; a desire for authority and rules, but also for recognition and appreciation; work and performance; conformism and risk avoidance;*

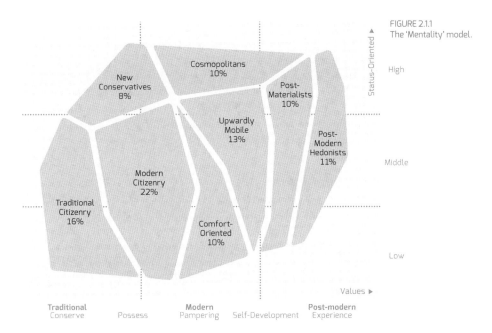

FIGURE 2.1.1
The 'Mentality' model.

materialistic and status conscious; technology minded; traditional
division of roles; equal percentage of men and women; relatively low
education.

### Comfort-Oriented, 10%
Impulsive and passive consumers whose main focus is on a stress-free,
pleasant and comfortable lifestyle
*Keywords: be free and live an easy life; pleasure-oriented; not interested
in society and politics; desire for recognition and appreciation; no
certitudes or responsibilities; impulsive; living in and for the here and
now; materialistic and consumption-oriented; geared towards outward
appearances; individualistic; more women than men; fewer old people,
more people with low education.*

### New Conservatives, 8%
The liberal-conservative upper layer of society who are keen to promote
technological development, but resist social and cultural innovation.
*Keywords: hanging onto traditional norms and values; protection of
social status; interest in politics and history; work and performance;
sober; risk avoidance; insistence on good manners; central role of family
relationships; more men than women; more elderly; more people with
high education; more people with high incomes.*

### Upwardly Mobile, 13%
Career-oriented individualists with a strong fascination for social
status, new technologies, risk and stress.
*Keywords: build a career; free of tradition and obligations; open to
innovation and change; international orientation; materialistic and
status-conscious; technology minded; impulsive and adventurous;
orientated around kindred spirits; more men than women; relatively high
percentage of younger people.*

**Post-Materialistic, 10%**

Idealists, social critics with a wish for self-development who denounce social injustice and stand up for the environment.

*Keywords: solidarity and social engagement; awareness of immaterial values; tolerant; international orientation; people who search for a balance between work and private life; play constructive role in society; not consumption and amusement-oriented; partners have own friends; more women than men; somewhat higher age bracket; more people with high educational levels.*

**Post-Modern Hedonists, 11%**

The pioneers of the experience culture, in which experiment and the breaching of moral and social conventions have become targets in themselves.

*Keywords: freedom; little societal and political engagement; equal opportunities; impulsive; adventurous; no commitments; oriented towards experience; individualistic; friends more important than family; equal percentages of men and women; more young people; more people with high education.*

**Cosmopolitans, 10%**

Open and critical citizens of the world who integrate post-modern values, such as the development of their own talents and experience, into modern values such as social success, materialism and hedonism.

*Keywords: self-development; international orientation; social and political awareness; ambition; materialistic and technology minded; impulsive and adventurous; status-conscious; well-mannered; networker; oriented towards peers and kindred spirits; equal percentages of men and women; more young people; more people with high incomes.*

## 2.2 Measuring Instruments

This section describes the history of efforts to measure aesthetics.

### 2.2.1 Bense (1954): *Aesthetica, Metaphysische Beobachtungen am Schönen*

In the years shortly before and after World War II a number of efforts were made to measure when an object (of art), a design or a building is beautiful or ugly. In his book *Aesthetica* Max Bense tried to find formulas for beauty in art, in technology and in nature.

$$Ks = (W + [Cw \cdot N']) \cdot M$$
$$Ts = (W + [Cw \cdot N]) \cdot M$$
$$Ns = W + Cw$$

The abbreviations in these formulas have the following meaning.
*Ks:   beauty in art*

**Ts**:  *beauty in technology*
**Ns**:  *beauty in nature*
**W**:  *reality*
**Cw**: *environment*
**N**:  *necessity*
**N'**: *non-necessity (the opposite of necessity)*
**M**:  *possibility*

Bense did not manage to develop his formulas in any further detail. He only gives some reflections on them. In his book he refers to the formula used by Birkhoff (1928) for the aesthetic measure (M):

$$M = \frac{C}{O}$$

In this formula O stands for the measure of order of the object and C for the complexity. According to Bense, this formula can be used only for objects or designs that are not too complex ('möglichst einfache, nicht zusammengestelte ästhetische Objekte' (Bense, 1954, pp. 31-32)). The main problem with all the formulas described is that concepts on both sides of the '=' sign cannot be filled in with numbers.

## 2.2.2   Berlyne (1971): *Aesthetics and Psychobiology*

Berlyne (1971) started his research to try and establish why people are interested in objects – such as works of art – that do not seem to have any biological benefit for them. According to Berlyne, people search (actively) for stimuli that trigger their senses in the right way. If the design is too easy or too complex to comprehend, it will be judged more negatively. The aesthetic appreciation of a pattern depends on the extent to which it can stimulate the senses. The graphic representation of this phenomenon has a reversed U-form. Patterns or designs with a level of interest that is too low do not stimulate the senses and are therefore not pleasing, although not unpleasant either. In the words of Berlyne they are indifferent. If the level of interest intensifies, for instance because the pattern becomes more complex or because it contains unexpected irregularities, the level of interest grows and the senses are stimulated in a positive way. This continues until the pattern becomes too complicated and the observer starts to dislike it. In that case the senses are stimulated in a negative way, and the observer will find the pattern (or design) unpleasant (not beautiful, ugly).

There are three kinds of variables that can stimulate the senses:
- Physiological aspects, such as size of the object, intensity, hue and saturation of colours.
- Ecological aspects, such as learned or associative meaning of a picture or object.
- Comparative properties, such as newness, ambiguity, contradiction and complexity.

Berlyne's research concentrated on the last category. He found

FIGURE 2.2.1
Pleasantness versus
complexity.

FIGURE 2.2.2
Interestingness versus
complexity.

a reversed U-form, which reflected the relationship between aesthetic
appreciation and complexity (as shown in Figure 2.2.1), ambiguity,
irregularity and/or newness (originality), where uniformity, order and
familiarity would lower the level of interest and variation, complexity
and newness would enhance the level of interest. Whether an increase
in the level of interest is experienced as positive depends on the level of
enhancement, the situation and the experience of the beholder. Berlyne
adds that the appreciation for complexity rises with both age and the
level of artistic training or education of the subjects. Over the years
Berlyne's model has been quite widely disputed. Some researchers did
not agree with his reversed U-form, but instead advocated a linear,
rising line (as shown in Figure 2.2.2). It also seems as if Berlyne's model
works best for simple, artificially created designs. The model does not
work so well as soon as the designs, such as paintings, have an associative or learned meaning.

In later research Berlyne made a distinction between 'pleasantness'
and 'interestingness'. According to these new insights, simple, easy-to-
understand, redundant patterns are found to be pleasing, but a pattern
is considered interesting only if it contains some disorientation that
cannot be understood within seconds, but instead requires the observer
to take a second look. Interestingness grows in a linear manner with
complexity, whereas pleasantness gives a reversed U-form: not enough
complexity is boring, too much complexity is annoying.

### 2.2.3 Boselie (1982): *Over Visuele Schoonheidservaring*

Boselie researched what aspects of patterns lead to aesthetic appreciation.
He distinguishes between aesthetic, hedonistic and affective values that
an object (or a piece of art or music) can have for the observer. According
to Boselie, hedonistic value is more extensive than aesthetic value.

We speak of a positive hedonistic value if the experience is pleasant,
joyful. We speak of a negative hedonistic value if the experience is
unpleasant, inconvenient. *(Boselie, 1982, p. 2)*

From earlier research it can be concluded, according to Boselie, that
stimuli are considered pleasant or unpleasant for various reasons.
Subjects give qualifications such as beautiful, funny, interesting and
exciting or, by contrast, ugly, boring and farfetched. It was found that
the stimulus that was considered to be the most beautiful was often

not considered to be the most exciting. The qualifications mentioned above describe the affective meaning of the stimuli. They are measured on what is called a semantic scale. That is a scale on which the subjects judge a stimulus on opposite qualifications, such as beautiful/ugly, small/big or exciting/boring. Often the subjects can choose from a scale of five or seven steps.

In his research Boselie uses two-dimensional patterns that consist of lines and dots. In short, his results can be summarized as follows: perceptual beauty is directly related to perceptual order. The perception of beauty is directly related to the experience of order perceived by the subject. If a pattern consists of a combination of different orders, the experience of beauty will grow if the perception of order is stronger, and will diminish if the order is hard to perceive.

Even in his introduction Boselie remarks that, in empirical research into art, the statements of subjects are often considered to be typical for the subject, not for the work of art. He therefore concludes his thesis with a discussion of ecological validity. Because the situation in a laboratory differs from reality, one can question whether the results are still valid in the real world. If it is difficult to draw conclusions in daily life based on the experiments in a laboratory, one speaks of a low ecological validity. According to Boselie, many researchers and authors doubt the validity of experiments with regard to aesthetics. Arguments that these critics use are as follows:
- The patterns offered to the subjects are of a kind that no one in their right mind would examine for longer than a fraction of a second (outside the experimental situation in which he 'has to' look).
- The situations in which the subjects examine the patterns are very different from real life situations. The subjects are asked to give an aesthetic judgement, but there is a substantial chance that the subjects instead try to show off their artistic expertise rather than to give their personal opinion.

In response to this, Boselie argues that some pieces of art – he mentions Kandinsky, Liberman, Struycken – strongly resemble the patterns he used in his experiments.

He also states that the hypotheses that he considers to have 'partially proved' – meaning that perceived beauty equals perceived order – are valid mainly for simple patterns. However, he does not exclude that in more complex patterns as well, such as in baroque, the patterns that have the highest perceived order – within the rules of the style – will be considered to be the most beautiful.

Boselie's research can also be regarded as an argument for large-scale variation. Although in his experiments he finds a majority of subjects that confirm his hypotheses, there is also always a substantial minority (of sometimes up to 40%) that do not agree and choose the other design. (In Boselie's experiments the designs are compared 'pair wise'.) This is a minority that many marketers would find very interesting if it repre-sented the possible market share.

### 2.2.4 Hekkert (1995): *Artful Judgements*

In his research into aesthetic preference for visual patterns Hekkert distinguishes four influential factors.

**Physiological Properties**
Physiological properties are the objective and quantifiable properties of pieces of art or designs, such as measures (length, width, stroke width), arcs, planes, colours (hue, brightness, saturation), textures.

**Organization**
The organization of the features, the way the elements are organized to create harmony, unity, balance, homogeneity or, on the other hand, complexity, absurdity, variety and heterogeneity.

**Meaning**
The qualities that give meaning to an object, such as semantic meaning, reference to an archetype, associative meaning, etc.

**Denotation**
The meaning of a work of art is denotative if the work refers to an (historic) event.

Hekkert excludes emotional meaning (emotional benefits) from his study. In the introduction to his research he distinguishes objective and subjective theories. Objective studies suppose that aesthetic judgements are not dependent on the background, level of education, or experience of the observer of the work of art. On the other hand, subjective theories suppose that the observer's background does have some influence. According to the first group, there should be some kind of 'objective aesthetic truth'. According to the subjective theories, there will only be a joint aesthetic meaning if the background, education and experience of the observers are comparable, if they belong to the same social group, or if they judge under comparable circumstances. He quotes Hume as an example of an 'extreme' subjective theory. According to Hume, beauty is not a quality of an object or a work of art, but only exists in the mind of the observer. Every observer has a different aesthetic judgement. It is most likely that Hekkert is referring here to the statement: 'Beauty is in the eye of the beholder'. Opinions differ regarding the real source of this statement: 'The first appearance of this phrase seems to have been in Molly Bawn, 1878, a novel about a frivolous, flirtatious Irish girl. The novel was written by Margaret Wolfe Hungerford (Hamilton) (1855-1897)' (The Phrase Finder, 2011; Yahoo Answers, 2011).

Hekkert describes three groups of theories about aesthetic reviews that partly overlap. The first group – the theory of Berlyne is an example – examines the stimulation of the senses and may have a kind of common conclusion, namely that not enough stimulation of the senses is boring, too much stimulation results in rejection, with aesthetic appreciation lying somewhere in between. The second group looks at the familiarity with the 'rules' of the observer. The phenomena that play a role appear to be similar to those of the first group. Excessive proximity to the archetype (being seen too often) is not very exciting, and an excessive difference from the archetype is not recognized (does not belong to the archetype) and is therefore not appreciated. Appreciation is based on a differentiation with the archetype that is not excessive, but still sufficiently surprising. The third group of theories adds that the observer's degree of expertise plays an important role in the observations.

## 2.3  Behaviouristic Explanations

### 2.3.1   Crilly et al. (2004): *Seeing Things: Consumer Response to the Visual Domain in Product Design*

This study discusses consumer responses to product visual form with an emphasis on the aesthetic, semantic and symbolic aspects of the cognitive response to design (Figure 2.3.1). In this section a selection is made of those aspects that are the most relevant for designers and that are related to Evolutionary Product Development. Products are considered to be signs that can be interpreted by users. A consumer can react to a product by cognition and an affect that may be followed by behaviour.

### Cognition
The first – cognition – can be described using the following categories: aesthetic impression, semantic interpretation, and symbolic association.

**Aesthetic Impression**
According to Coates (2003), the aesthetic impression is the result of two factors, namely information and concinnity (Berlyne, 1971, proposes pleasure and interest, see Section 2.2.2). He suggests that both stem from the objective qualities of a product and from the subjective experiences of the consumer. This leads to four components of aesthetic impression: Objective information, Subjective information, Objective concinnity and Subjective concinnity.
-  Objective information concerns the degree of contrast that a product presents against competing products, the environment in which it is used and (the complexity of) its design.
-  Subjective information is the novelty perceived in the product by the consumer. A design that is completely new to one consumer may be quite familiar to a more experienced consumer.
-  Objective concinnity is related to the order that can be perceived in the product (e.g. symmetry).
-  Subjective concinnity refers to the extent to which the product is understood by the consumer. Aspects are the cultural background of the consumer and the degree of commonality with products that are known to him.

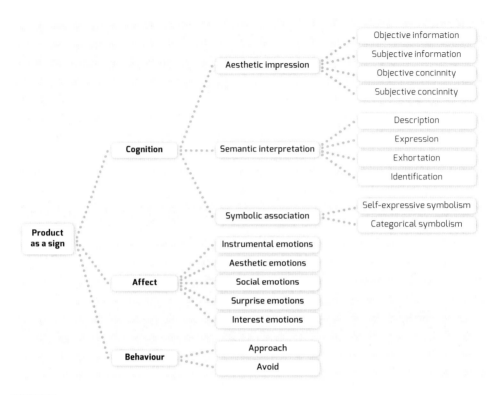

```
                                              Objective information

                                              Subjective information
                     Aesthetic impression
                                              Objective concinnity

                                              Subjective concinnity

                                              Description

                                              Expression
    Cognition        Semantic interpretation
                                              Exhortation

                                              Identification

                                              Self-expressive symbolism
                     Symbolic association
                                              Categorical symbolism

                     Instrumental emotions

                     Aesthetic emotions
Product
as a sign    Affect  Social emotions

                     Surprise emotions

                     Interest emotions

                     Approach
             Behaviour
                     Avoid
```

FIGURE 2.3.1
An overview of the aspects that involve consumer response to product visual form according to Crilly et al.

Coates suggests that these four factors are items on a weighing scale:

If information outweighs concinnity, the product will be considered confusing, meaningless and ugly. Alternatively, if concinnity outweighs information, the product will be considered simple, dull and boring. *(Crilly et al., 2004, p. 558)*

This principle seems related to the famous MAYA principle – Most Advanced Yet Acceptable – of Raymond Loewy:

The adult public's taste is not necessarily ready to accept the logical solutions to their requirements if the solution implies too vast a departure from what they have been conditioned into accepting as the norm.  *(Loewy, 2011)*

### Semantic Interpretation
In the description of semantic interpretation, Crilly et al. use Monö's semantic functions (Monö, 1997): Description, Expression, Exhortation and Identification.
- Description refers to the way a product is self-explanatory, the way its form explains its use (without the need for instructions).
- Expression has to do with the way that the properties of the product are perceived. The design can show the user that it needs to be handled with care or that it is very robust and can withstand some abuse.

- Exhortation refers to the interaction between the user and the product. For example, a sound may draw the attention of a user that an action has to be undertaken.
- Identification is about the origin and affiliation of a product: the brand, product type, specific model, etc.

**Symbolic Association**
Products – but also behaviour, jewellery or make-up – are used by consumers to express themselves, for example to show that they are unique and/or that they belong to a group: Self-expressive symbolism and Categorical symbolism. Consumers use Self-expressive symbolism to try and express their individual qualities and differentiate themselves from other people around them. By contrast, they use Categorical symbolism to try and express the fact that they belong to a certain group or social class.

According to Crilly et al., the three cognitive responses to product design do not operate independently, but are highly interrelated:

For example, assessment of what a product is (Semantic interpreta-tion), may influence judgements on the elegance of a design (Aesthetic impression) and the social values it may connote (Symbolic associa-tion).   (Crilly et al., 2004, p. 564)

## Affect
Affect relates to the emotional responses that products may elicit. Desmet (2003) proposes five aspects: instrumental, aesthetic, social, surprise, and interest emotions.
- Instrumental emotions refer to the functioning of the product: is it pleasant to work with?
- Aesthetic emotions relate to the liking or disliking of a product based on its looks.
- Social emotions relate to what other people (may) think of the product.
- Surprise emotions relate to the novelty of the design in the eyes of the beholder.
- Interest emotions refer to the degree to which the consumer wants to possess and use the product.

## Behaviour
Behaviour is about the way consumers respond to a product. This aspect is not given much attention in the paper by Crilly et al. They distinguish between Approach or Avoid:

Approach responses may be associated with further investigation of the product, product purchase and product use. Avoid responses may be associated with ignoring the product, failure to purchase and even hiding the product.   (Crilly et al., 2004, p. 554)

## 2.4  Hierarchical Structures

The behaviour of groups is studied in Demographic Models (Section 2.1) and in the Measuring Instruments (Section 2.2) an attempt is made to find some kind of 'absolute truth', while the Behaviouristic Explanations (Section 2.3) concentrate on the psychology of human beings. In the Hierarchical Structures (Section 2.4) the focus is on the development stages that follow one another and/or exist simultaneously.

### 2.4.1  Maslow (1954/1976): *Motivation and Personality*

The American clinical psychologist, Abraham Maslow, distinguishes between five levels of human needs, which he describes as follows:

**1. Physiological Needs**
Food, water, sleep, homeostasis, sex and air to breathe: to live

**2. Safety Needs**
Safety, protection, need for structure, order, laws and borders; security of employment; freedom of fear, tension and chaos; health, property.

**3. Love and Belonging**
Belonging to a group or family, someone to love, a partner or children.

**4. Esteem**
A stable, firm founded, usually high self-esteem; self-respect; respect for others.
a.  achievement, competence, confidence vis-à-vis the world, independence and freedom.
b.  desire for reputation or prestige, standing, fame and glory, dominance, acknowledgement, attention, importance, dignity or appreciation.

**5. Need for Self-Actualization**
According to Maslow, self-actualizing leads to a different way of life and a different opinion about life. Self-actualized people are capable of understanding the heart of matters. They accept their environment, the people that surround them and themselves as they are, without feelings of guilt. They are able to recognize untruthful behaviour. They can see things in perspective. They have no fear of the unknown. They are more interested in the problems of their surroundings and of the world, instead of worrying continuously about their 'own little problems'. They form their own opinions and do not allow others to tell them what they should believe or think. They do not depend on adoration, status, income, popularity and prestige. They do not need expensive artefacts to show to the outside world. They feel responsible and emphasize with other (human) beings and nature. They transcend the egocentric way of life that is typical for Maslow's fourth level of needs. The fact that they have gone beyond this level probably explains why they are capable of seeing it. Self-actualizing people are far from perfect, and can be weary, stubborn or annoying. They are often vain, proud, arrogant and impatient. They are capable of – unexpected – ruthlessness (they not only form their own opinions themselves [as mentioned above],

but sometimes put their ideas into practice without much empathy for others).

According to the theory of Maslow, higher needs can be satisfied only if the needs at a lower level are more or less satisfied.
- A satisfied need does not motivate. If a need is satisfied to a certain extent, the motivation to satisfy it slowly disappears.
- Lower levels of need must be satisfied before motivation to a higher level is possible.
- When lower levels are satisfied, there is an automatic motivation towards the next higher level.

## 2.4.2 Woodring (1987): *Retailing New Product or Design*

During the 'Design Congress '87' in Amsterdam, Cooper Woodring presented an interesting theory on the hierarchy of products based on the history of retail in the USA. Before 1900 – according to Woodring – products were sold in small shops that were spread all over the cities and neighbourhoods. After 1900, department stores were built so that different, small shops could combine their activities under one roof. Around 1930, bakers, butchers, greengrocers and delicatessens started offering their products in one shop, and this is how supermarkets came about. They became a huge success, partly because of the increase in the number of cars that greatly enhanced people's mobility. Around 1950, discount stores were started that offered low-priced brand products because of their volumes and the principle of self-service.

### 'Wants' and 'Needs'

Woodring distinguishes four product categories that all need their own selling strategy and their own kind of shop. He starts with a division into 'wants' and 'needs'. Needs are products that we use on a daily basis. Wants are products that make life more pleasant. Many products start as wants and become needs some time later. An example of such a product is the refrigerator, once a product for rich people, now a commodity in every Western household.

Wants can be subdivided into lifestyle products and specialist products. Needs can be divided into service products and (fast moving) consumer products.

### Lifestyle Products

Lifestyle products are new, desirable, fashionable and exciting. They offer satisfaction and status. Examples are jewellery, clothing, furniture and art. They can be bought in shopping malls which house lots of shops within close reach of each other. International examples are: Maxfield (Los Angeles), KaDeWe (Berlin), GUM (Moscow) or Siam Paragon (Bangkok). Alternatively, you can find them in warehouses. The people who want to buy them are not in any hurry to do so. They might even decide not to buy there and then, but to try and do so at another time and place. It is good for all parties, both buyers and sellers, if there is a wide range as regards choice and price in a small area.

### Specialty Products

Specialty products promise the user good performance and are often technologically high-quality (high technology). Examples are products for sports, cameras, computers, audio-visual products, some glasses and lenses, smartphones and hobby products. They often need well-educated sellers that have (technological) knowledge. The potential buyers research the products using brochures, websites, articles in magazines and by exchanging information with peers. These products can be found in specialty shops and warehouses.

### Service Products

Service products start their economic life cycle as lifestyle products, then become specialty products and end up as service products. Sometimes they are free-standing products that change into fitments. Examples are heating, ventilation, air conditioning, bath, shower, domestic appliances (vacuum cleaner, irons, coffee machines) or tools (drilling machines). Because they often do not have (or no longer have) unique selling points, no differentiating features of design, consumers often do not have a brand preference. Therefore, these products are often sold via discounters. Some products are bought with a service contract.

### Fast-Moving Consumer Goods

Consumer goods are needed on a daily basis. Examples are food, beverages, cleaning products, medicines, fuels, and newspapers or magazines. They are bought routinely and frequently. Usually they are not very expensive (per unit). Often people buy well-known brands that are heavily advertised. In almost all cases the products are bought in the nearest available shop. Often that is a supermarket, or (for example in the USA and France) a hypermarket or convenience store.

A product can be presented in all four of the above-mentioned categories and can be sold via all the market channels that have been discussed, to both consumers and professional users. Woodring describes the camera as an example (please note that this example was given in 1987). A 'coloured, yellow disc-camera with funky product graphics and a suiting wrist bag' is a lifestyle product and will be sold in a shopping mall or department store. A Nikon with 35-mm lens is a specialty product and will be sold in a specialty shop. A security camera for a bank is a service product and will be sold with a service contract. A preloaded panorama camera is a consumer product and will be sold in a supermarket near the cashier.

## Woodring's Hierarchy

In 1920 the volume of products that were sold was related to price: the lower the price, the higher the volume (see Figure 2.4.1). Around 1950 this changed. People had more money to spend and did not always want to buy the cheapest product. The volume was then somewhere in the middle. There had to be a cheap, expensive and medium-priced version of each product. The latter category contained the greatest volume of products sold. Adding a high-priced new product raised the

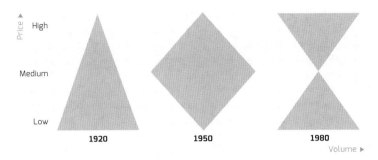

FIGURE 2.4.1
The number of products sold
(horizontal) versus their price
(vertical) in three periods.

attractiveness of the product 'in the middle'.

This strategy became very unprofitable for a number of companies around 1980 because of the 'enhancement sacrificial purchase syndrome', which can be summed up as follows.

I buy my clothes in a discount shop, flew tourist class to a conference in Amsterdam, stopped my subscription to pay TV and decided not to buy the essential new furniture so that I can buy a Hasselblad camera with Carl Zeiss lenses for $10,000.

According to Woodring, this is a clear example of the 'enhancement sacrificial purchase syndrome' that formed the basis for a change in people's purchasing behaviour around 1980. It was also a consequence of the worldwide recession at the time. The outcome was that the volume of purchases was no longer associated with the medium-priced category, but in the extremes. The diamond shape changed into an hourglass shape. It is not difficult to understand what this meant for manufacturers that were still using the diamond-shaped model: They consequently took the wrong products out of the market and introduced new products with the wrong pricing.

### 2.4.3  Rogers (1995): *Diffusion of Innovations*

In his book entitled *Diffusion of Innovations*, Rogers describes how new products are generally introduced. At that time, over 4,000 studies had been carried out. Rogers concludes, on the basis of this large number of studies, that the acceptance of product introductions generally follows a well-defined pattern. The most important variation within this pattern is the amount of time it takes between the introduction and the moment of complete acceptance. This can vary from a few years to a few centuries. According to Rogers' definition, a product is accepted if at least 90% of the potential users own the product. The market penetration of a product is about 50%, if it is owned by what he calls the 'innovators', the 'early adopters' and the 'early majority'. He adds that 'status' is one of the important motivations of these three groups.

Status motivations for adoption seem to be more important for innovators, early adopters, and early majority, and less important for the late majority and laggards.   *(Rogers, 1995, p.214)*

According to Rogers, the first buyers of new products are the 'innovators'. They are followed by the 'early adopters' and the 'early majority'. If these three groups own the product, the market penetration will be about 50%. The 'early majority' is followed by what he calls the 'late majority'. This is followed – if at all – by the 'laggards'. Rogers provides descriptions of the most important lifestyle characteristics and values of each of the adoption categories. After each category he indicates the percentage of people who suit his description.

### Innovators ('Venturesome'), 2.5%

Innovators are very interested in new ideas, new techniques and new products. They have 'cosmopolite social relationships' and plenty of contacts with other innovators, who sometimes live a long way away from them. They are capable of understanding (technological) complicated products, and have enough money to spend on them. They are able to live with the uncertainty that a new product can sometimes fail and do not mind if it does not function perfectly all the time. They look for new, cutting-edge, sometimes even dangerous, experiences. (They have a 'desire for the rash, the daring and the risky'). They can easily handle disappointments. However, they are not highly respected in their immediate social circle. They are often regarded as being rather eccentric.

### Early Adopters ('Respected'), 13.5%

Early adopters are much better integrated into their local community than innovators. They have a lot of prestige and authority but are less internationally oriented. Their opinion is highly valued. They are 'the individual to check with'.

### Early Majority ('Deliberate'), 34%

People that belong to the early majority have plenty of social contacts but are seldom opinion makers ('not the first by which the new is tried, nor the last to lay the old aside').

### Late Majority ('Sceptical'), 34%

The late majority will implement an innovation or buy a product only after it has been generally accepted and functions reliably. They often make decisions based on economic or technological need (the old system is no longer supported) or under pressure of their surroundings. They are sceptical towards innovations and careful in their decisions.

### Laggards ('Traditional'), 16%

Laggards have a small social network or are sometimes quite isolated. Their point of reference is the past: we have been doing things like this all the time, why would we suddenly want to change that? They often communicate only with people who share their opinion, they do not trust innovations, need a long time to come to a conclusion and often lack the means to afford an innovation that may prove to be a failure.

### 2.4.4  Christensen (1997): *the Innovator's Dilemma*

Christensen states that, when trying to predict the future, specialists usually do not do much more than extrapolate the present:

[…] The only thing we may know for sure when we read expert's forecasts about how large emerging markets will become is that they are wrong.  *(Christensen, 1997, p. xxi)*

He differentiates between two kinds of innovations, sustaining and disruptive innovations.

### Sustaining and Disruptive Innovations

Why do well-organized and well-managed companies that seem to do what they should do, fail? They listen carefully to the wishes of their clients, they introduce new technologies as soon as possible, they strive for better products for a lower price and they produce what their customers want.

In his book *The Innovator's Dilemma,* Christensen (1997) provides the following explanation as to why such companies fail. The fact that they listened to their clients, invested in the latest technologies, offered their clients better performing products, that is products that met the needs of their clients better, based their developments on careful and thorough research of trends in the market and invested in the markets that promised the best financial results was the reason why they lost their market leadership.

In his study he concludes that it sometimes makes sense not to listen to clients, but to invest in products that perform not in line with the wishes of these clients and that have a lower profit margin. He also concludes that it is sometimes better to invest in small, not very interesting, markets rather than in big, much more promising markets.

Most of the time innovations are sustaining. A sustaining innovation is one that fulfils a desire held by existing clients. Often this means improving the performance of the product. Sustaining innovations hardly ever lead to the failure of an organization. A sustaining innovation leads to an improved product with an immediate, positive result for the company. The company's clients ask for the improvement and immediately buy it.

In the event of a disruptive innovation there is, according to Christensen, no improvement of the product that the existing relations are interested in. On the contrary, the present clients will not want the innovation. Disruptive innovations have to find an own, new market. The problem for the present organization comes later, after the product has been developed in more detail, and sometimes only after several years, when the disruptive innovation has been improved in such a way that it has become interesting to their clients. In many cases it is then too late. The new organization will have acquired such a strong position in the market that the existing organizations are unable to catch up.

A disruptive innovation is a competitive product that is cheaper than the existing products and that performs less well. The market for the product is small and therefore not interesting for the existing suppliers. Disruptive innovations usually fulfil most of the following criteria:
- The products are simpler in the sense that they perform less well and offer fewer possibilities.
- The products are cheaper.
- The profits are lower.
- The products are successful in small, uninteresting markets.
- The key clients of the present producers do not want the product (and usually have no use for it either).

### 2.4.5 Pine and Gilmore (1999): *the Experience Economy*

In their book *The Experience Economy*, Pine and Gilmore distinguish between the following four phases for products and services:
- Commodity
- Good
- Service
- Experience

According to them 'commodities' are taken from raw and basic materials. They are very similar, and that makes price the main means of competition. As examples they refer to coffee beans, crude oil and cereals. If a company burns, grinds and packages coffee beans, it makes what Pine and Gilmore call a 'good'. Although it can demand a better price than if it sold only burned coffee beans, the level of competition means its price cannot be set very high. 'Services' are aimed at individuals. Service products use goods to create services for their clients. A hairdresser uses – amongst other things – scissors, combs and a hairdryer to cut and style his clients' hair. A gardener needs a complete set of tools and machines to construct and maintain someone's garden. According to Pine and Gilmore, people are more interested in services than in goods and are therefore willing to pay more for them. They call the fourth level 'experience'. Companies that offer an experience use their products and their services to commit the customer. They explain this as follows:

While commodities are fungible, goods tangible, and services intangible, experiences are memorable.   *(Pine and Gilmore, 1999, pp. 11-12)*

It is the memory that makes an experience stand out while, in general, commodities, goods and services are soon forgotten.

### 2.4.6 Jordan (2000): *Designing Pleasurable Products, an Introduction to the New Human Factors*

According to Jordan, features such as the usability of a product start as – what in marketing terminology is referred to as – satisfiers. Later, however, they come to be expected and this transforms them into dissatisfiers if they are not included in the product. He identifies three hierarchical levels of human factors.

- level 1: Functionality
- level 2: Usability
- level 3: Pleasure

Each level is a satisfier until most of the products have reached a certain quality. From that moment on, the lack of enough functionality or usability causes them to become dissatisfiers.

## Four Pleasures

At the third level – Pleasure – Jordan distinguishes four different types. The first is Physio-pleasure, which refers to touch (think of a pen or an electric shaver), taste or smell (the first thing some people do when they have bought a new book is open it and smell it). Then comes what he calls Socio-pleasure. This concerns pleasure derived from relationships with other people, and is accompanied by questions such as, 'Does the product suit me or what does the product say about me?' The next pleasure is Psycho-pleasure, which refers to the emotions felt by experiencing the product. The product is, for instance, 'fun to use'. Finally he refers to Ideo-pleasure (ideological pleasure), which refers to the value a product has for its owner.

Although the Four Pleasure model gives some insight into the emotional aspects of products, it is very difficult to separate them. For instance, Jordan states that a product made of a biodegradable material embodies the value of environmental responsibility and is therefore an example of Ideo-pleasure. However, this characteristic can also offer the owner Psycho-pleasure (the product is emotionally satisfying because of this material) or Socio-pleasure (people will see me as responsible and environment friendly because of this product).

## 2.5  Other Relevant Research

In this section a number of studies are discussed that are relevant to Evolutionary Product Development, but which do not fit in one of the above-mentioned themes.

### 2.5.1  Forty (1986): *Objects of Desire*

In his book *Objects of Desire*, Adrian Forty provides an interesting vision of the sometimes lengthy existence of styles and the lack of generally applicable scientific theories in the world of (industrial) design. He concludes that most books that have been written about design primarily offer descriptions of the life and work of (well-known) designers.

It seems odd that the biographies of individuals should be considered a satisfactory means of explaining an activity that is by nature social and not purely personal [...] If political economy consisted only of the study of the economy in the light of the statements made by politicians, the subject would indeed do little to increase our understanding of the world. Clearly, it would be foolish to dismiss designers' statements altogether, but we should not expect them to reveal all there is to know about design.   *(Forty, 1986, p. 239)*

In books about design and industrial design engineering the created designs are, in most cases, based on the career, the statements, ideas and theories of individual designers. No consideration is given to things such as the wants and needs of consumers, the price of the product, the market segment that the products were aimed at, or the way they were advertised. In this vision the existence of products is considered only to be the result of the creativity of the designer. This way of looking at products is misleading and ignores the fact that a lot more needs to be done to launch a successful product onto the market than just design work.

Although designers prepare designs, the responsibility for carrying them out rests with the entrepreneur; in the development of a manufactured article, it is normal for many preliminary designs to be prepared, from which one is chosen by the entrepreneur to be worked up for production.   *(Forty, 1986, p. 241)*

In most cases the entrepreneur will chose from several concepts created by the designer. Although a designer may give his opinion on the concept that should be chosen, it is rare for him to be the decision maker.

Many designers will admit that when they put up their first proposals, the entrepreneur chose a different design from the one they themselves favoured, and that it was the entrepreneur's choice and not their own on which the development went ahead. It is the entrepreneur not the designer who decides which design most satisfactorily embodies the ideas necessary to the product's success, and which best fits the material conditions of production.   *(Forty, 1986, p. 241)*

However, because designers usually only talk and write about what they themselves do, design is often considered to be a process that is completely controlled by them. According to Forty, this is even what is sometimes taught at design schools. One consequence is that some students get a completely wrong impression of what they can achieve. Another may be that they become frustrated in their later career.

[...] students are liable to acquire grandiose illusions about the nature of their skills, with the result that they become frustrated in their subsequent careers.   *(Forty, 1986, p. 241)*

### 2.5.2  Krishnan and Ulrich (2001): *Product Development Decisions: a Review of the Literature*

The paper by Krishnan and Ulrich provides an overview of the literature relating to research into product development. The research focuses on research within firms, which means that it, for example, excludes market developments, or governmental rules and regulations. It includes the organizational process (within the firm): e.g. the structure and organization of the design team, operations management (e.g. supplier and material selection, production sequence and project management), marketing (product positioning and pricing, collecting and meeting customer needs) and engineering design (product performance, size, configuration and dimensions).

In their research, product development is divided into four categories, namely concept development, product design, supply-chain design, and production ramp-up and launch. In their concluding remarks they state:

We noted that there is essentially no academic research on industrial design, the activity largely concerned with the form and style of products. Yet aesthetic design may be one of the most important factors in explaining consumer preference in some product markets, including automobiles, small appliances, and furniture.   *(Krishnan and Ulrich, 2001, pp. 14)*

### 2.5.3   Prahalad and Ramaswamy (2004): *the Future of Competition: Co-Creating Value with Customers*

A development that attracted a great deal of interest around the turn of the century is co-creation. Co-creation is defined as the active and direct involvement of users in the development of new products. The advantage for companies is that it gives them a better insight into the wishes and ideas of users. The advantage for consumers is that it gives them products that are better attuned to their individual wishes.

Prahalad and Ramaswamy (2004) suggest that the interest in co-creation is based primarily on the availability of information. Thanks to smartphones and the internet, consumers have access to large amounts of information about companies, products, techniques, trends, etc. and can share this information very quickly. Therefore, it is no longer possible to operate anonymously. The new communication tools mean consumers can and will communicate with companies. Their power and influence will increase. Three forms of co-creation can be distinguished, namely in production, in final design and in the concept development.

**Co-Creation in the Production Phase**
In the production phase, consumers hardly have any influence on the end result, and most of the time, they are only involved in assembling the product. The advantages for the users are an often substantial cost reduction and the pride of authorship: 'I made it myself'. Examples are Ikea and many DIY products.

**Co-Creation in the Final Design**
In this case the consumer can choose from a (very) large number of possibilities and combinations. This is what is often called 'mass customization'. The consumer defines the final design – often via internet – with the aid of a toolkit. The main advantage for the user is that he owns a unique product. A disadvantage is that it sometimes takes a lot of time to learn to work with the sometimes complicated toolkit.

## Co-Creation in the Concept Phase

Co-creation in the concept phase of product design is often related to market research. The most important differences are that the participating consumers are the future users of the product and that they stay involved during the whole design process. In traditional market research they are only asked for their opinion, and it is uncertain whether any of this is used in the end result. There are different ways to organize co-creation in the concept phase. Companies sometimes organize 'co-creation workshops'. However, the participants in these workshops are often not the future users of the product. If that is the case, the workshops are not much more than a new form of market research. Sometimes the initiative is taken by consumers themselves. One reason may be that they are not satisfied with existing products. They can, for instance, form an internet community to develop a better product. According to Shah (2000) these communities are often formed by sports practitioners such as windsurfers, snowboarders or skateboarders. Another well-known example of a product developed by a community is the computer operating system Linux.

# 3 EVOLUTIONARY PRODUCT DEVELOPMENT

## 3.1 Conclusions Regarding Theories Related to Industrial Design Engineering

The research and theories described in Chapter 2 offer industrial designers few starting points for developing or styling new products. In a review of the literature on product development decisions, Krishnan and Ulrich (2001) (see also Section 2.5.2) conclude that:

[…] there is essentially no academic research on industrial design, the activity largely concerned with the form and style of products. Yet aesthetic design may be one of the most important factors in explaining consumer preference in some product markets, including automobiles, small appliances, and furniture.   *(Krishnan and Ulrich, 2001, pp. 14)*

An exhaustive overview of these aspects (aesthetic, semantic and symbolic aspects of design) is given by Crilly et al. (2004) (see also Section 2.3.1). Some conclusions of this overview match the theory presented in this study. They mention the appearance after some time of a dominant design (that they call a 'stereotype' or 'prototype'), and they agree with the conclusion that in mature markets product performance is taken for granted so that attention to design has to shift to 'emotional benefits'. They state in their overview that:

[…] very few of the scientific studies have led to generalizations which are useful for students or practitioners of design.   *(Crilly et al., 2004, pp. 559)*

Support for an evolutionary model of product development can be found in Berlyne (1971), Christensen (1997), Coates (2003), Crilly et al. (2004), Jordan (2000), Loewy (2011), Rogers (1995), and Woodring (1987). The best starting points for a model of Evolutionary Product Development can be found in the demographic models (Foot, 1996; Mitchell, 1983; Motivaction International, 2009; Veblen, 1899/1994) (Section 2.1) and hierarchical structures (Jordan, 2000; Maslow, 1954/1976; Pine and Gilmore, 1999; Rogers, 1995; Woodring, 1987) (Section 2.4). Several authors conclude that there is a certain hierarchy in the performance that users expect from products, and that there is a certain, fixed pattern in the way this hierarchy is arranged (Jordan, 2000; Pine and Gilmore, 1999; Rogers, 1995; Woodring, 1987).

Furthermore, Christensen (1997) gives a description of the phenomenon of 'disruptive innovations' that appears to be similar to the description of Rogers (1995) with regard to products that are attractive to people he calls 'innovators'. The theory of Foot (1996) and the models of Mitchell (1983) and Motivaction International (2009) offer starting points with regard to target groups, based on, amongst other things, demographic models and the wishes that users have with regard to products.

### 3.1.1    From Deterministic to Evolutionary Models

It is interesting to note that, at the end of the twentieth century, a deterministic starting point has slowly been replaced by an evolutionary one in a number of disciplines. Examples are economics and economic history (Freeman and Louçã, 2001; Nelson and Winter, 1982), technological developments (Ziman, 2000), psychology (Gaulin and McBurney, 2004) and processes of cultural change (McDonald Dunbar and Knight, 1999).

One example is the neoclassical equilibrium model from theoretical economics. The character of this model is deterministic. The model predicts that markets will reach an equilibrium between the economic subjects and the available means if all the sellers who want to sell at, or below, a given price sell to all the buyers who are willing to buy at, or above, a given price (among others: Yang, 2001). The mechanism behind this equilibrium functions in the same way as natural selection does in an evolutionary model. Only those products will survive that offer a maximum of (economical) satisfaction against the lowest possible price. Being 'adapted in the best possible way to the environment' is described in the neoclassical equilibrium model as 'the highest possible benefit for the lowest possible price'. Since, in the equilibrium model, competition runs completely blind, meaning that no individual subject can influence the result of the process, it is clear that the 'natural selection' in an evolutionary model and the 'completely blind' running in the deterministic equilibrium model perform the same function and work in the same direction.

If the two fundamentals of the model (those of complete information for all subjects and complete homogeneity of the competing products) are left out, the model loses its deterministic character and starts to look more and more like an evolutionary process (Nelson and Winter, 1982; Ormerod, 1994, 1998, 2005). The consequence of this is that concepts such as 'partial path dependency', 'embeddedness', 'technological lock-in' and 'dominant design' cannot be explained by the neoclassical model and are therefore considered to be 'anomalies'. However, they can be explained if an Evolutionary Product Development model is used as a framework. This constitutes an important reason to investigate in more detail the possibilities of an evolutionary vision on product development and innovation. For both industrial design engineers and economists the selection is the same, namely acceptance by the market. This principle can be used not only in evolutionary economics, but also in evolutionary product development.

It is possible to conclude that the performance of a new product shortly after its introduction will be low and that, at the start of its evolution, it is not yet clear what configuration will offer the best chances for survival and improvement of this performance (Christensen, 1997; Rogers, 1995). It can therefore be expected that different configurations will be introduced and tested on the market. The introduction of a new product will generally be based on a strategy that appears to be similar to trial and error and that will therefore have a lot in common with biological evolution. After a time one or more configurations will become successful in the market. Competitors will often respond by copying the successful products, either by launching them onto the market for a lower price or by improving them. Some of them will probably be successful because they do not have to earn back the original research and development costs. The competition at this stage of the economic life cycle of a product will be based on performance, with the strategies either being copying or slightly improving the successful products. After a while it will become clear that some variants can be improved more easily than others. The consequence will be that more and more competitors will use this variant, thereby taking the first step towards a 'dominant design'. It is still possible to improve the performance, but the steps that can be made decrease gradually. The consequence will be that new innovations will be aimed not only at the performance of the product, but also at the production and distribution. The dominant activities in this phase will be optimization of the product, the production, the distribution, the service etc.

After a while this strategy will also lose its effectiveness. The profits that can be made will become smaller when it is no longer possible to improve the margins by means of improved performance or an improved process. The only remaining strategy to keep or enlarge the market is to introduce the product on different markets. In this phase the product designer will start to concentrate his activities on segmentation. The products will be increasingly attuned to the target groups, as a consequence of which the submarkets will become smaller. The final result may be a market segment with one customer or, in other words, individualization (Prahalad and Ramaswamy, 2004). However, individualization is not possible for some products. An example is fuel for cars (petrol, diesel). Someone who needs fuel generally stops at the nearest petrol station without worrying about the brand being offered. This has led to two strategies. On the one hand, customers are offered an additional reason for choosing a brand, for instance by means of saving systems, which are quite popular in the Netherlands, or via a shop that offers other products (food, drinks, small souvenirs, etc.). The other strategy is 'corporate communication'. The importance of this communication, and the power that consumers have, was shown by the consumer pressure on Shell because of its decision to sink the drill platform Brent Spar in the ocean after negative press publicity.

It can be concluded that it seems as if an evolutionary model offers possibilities for explaining the development of products over time. The six product phases are described in more detail in Section 3.4.

## 3.2 Product Phases

As mentioned in the first chapter, a well-known method for analyzing the different phases of development of a product is the economic product life cycle (Figure 3.2.1). In this life cycle the turnover of a product is measured against time. Although the economic product life cycle is a key concept in product development and marketing, questions can be raised about its predictive value. If no unexpected events occur, the level of turnover may be predicted for a couple of years, but it is impossible to make predictions about the nature of product renewal or about users' demands and wishes. However, with the help of 'product phases' it is possible to make overall predictions as to the functionality, the design, the pricing, and the production of a product, as well as the level of service and the social behaviour of a company.

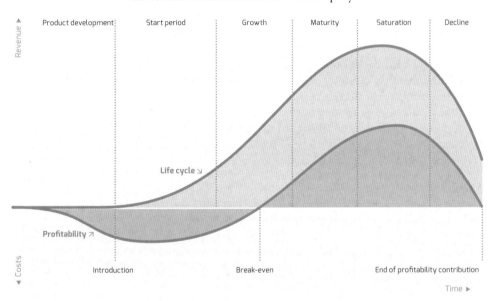

FIGURE 3.2.1
The economic product life cycle.

Theoretically, the economic product life cycle has six phases (Buijs and Valkenburg, 2000). The first phase, product development, shows the costs of the product before its introduction. Immediately after the introduction of the product, the pioneering phase starts (start period in Figure 3.2.1). If the product is accepted on the market, a phase of fast growth will begin, leading to increased turnover, which is the growth phase. In general, competition will occur during the growth phase. The next phase of the product life cycle is the maturity phase. Characteristics of this phase are a decrease in growth and the elimination of weaker competitors. During the next two phases, saturation and decline, turnover will first reach its peak, after which growth will start decreasing (e.g., because of substitute products coming onto the market). During the last phase, the product will almost completely disappear. Sometimes a residual market will remain and another phase will follow, referred to as ossification. Evidently, only a few products will follow this theoretical line. In addition, all kinds of external factors may influence the course of the line. For example, the mandatory wearing of safety belts in the back of cars may result in a doubling in the sales of safety belts during a short period of time.

This chapter summarizes the phenomena that appear during the phases of a product's life. These phenomena apply to, amongst other things, the market (is the product new to the market, or are there a lot of competitors?), the functionality (is it possible to improve the functionality or has it reached a high degree of perfection?), and the ergonomics (has enough attention been paid to the product's ease of use or is there scope for improvement?). The regularities that were found have been analyzed and described, and this led to the description of six product phases: performance, optimization, itemization, segmentation, individualization, and awareness. The six phases are placed in a chronological order so that any predictions about new or future products can be made. This can be done by positioning a product, based on its product characteristics, in one of the product phases. When developing a future product, a designer can add to the product characteristics of the next product phase, thereby creating added value for the intended user. In this way, the product phases can help a designer to create the next generation of a product.

## 3.3 Product Characteristics

The product phases are described by means of so-called product characteristics. Each product phase can be described in terms of eight product characteristics, four of which apply to the product itself and the others to its market, its production technology, the services that accompany it and the ethical aspects of the product in question.

The eight product characteristics are[3]
1. Newness
2. Functionality
3. Product development
4. Styling
5. Pricing
6. Production
7. Service
8. Ethics

---

3  In the original study (Eger, 2007) 10 product characteristics were proposed. However, in a later study (see Section 7.3) two of them proved to be statistically not significant. Both of them are most of the time not directed by designers. One of them, the number of competitors, is usually a given fact. The second, the way promotion is done, is in most cases not or only partially influenced by designers.

## 3.4 Description of the Product Phases

FIGURE 3.4.1
The six product phases.

We assert that each of the six product phases displays a typical pattern of product characteristics (Figure 3.4.1). In this section, the product characteristics are explained for each product phase.

### 3.4.1 Performance

New products – that is, products based on new technologies – normally suffer from teething troubles for some time when they first appear on the market. By implication, improving the primary functionality (i.e., the technical performance of the product) is the most important aspect of product development in this phase. Technically, new products often start as status symbols, and usually perform worse than the existing alternatives. The product characteristics of the product phase 'performance' can be summarized as follows. Technically speaking, the product is new and results from a 'technology push'. The performance of the product is often poor. Product development is primarily aimed at improving performance. Design in the limited sense of 'overall form giving' is unimportant and therefore product aesthetics are of minor concern. The product is often launched into the market by a monopolist or a small number of heterogeneous oligopolists, so competition is low. As a consequence, the price per unit can be relatively high. The product is frequently produced by standard machinery equipment, it often has more parts than the number that would be technically feasible, and assembly is mostly done by hand.

**Summary**
1. The product is new to the market and results from a 'technology push'.
2. The performance of the product is poor.
3. Product development is aimed at improving the performance.
4. Form giving is not very important, and therefore matching form giving to different parts of the product is poor (sometimes leading to a product that is not very aesthetically pleasing).
5. The price per unit is relative high.
6. The product is designed for production using standard machining, the product usually has many parts, and it is often assembled by hand.
7. There is no organized service organization. (This does not mean that there is no service, since start-up companies often offer a lot of service and support.)
8. The social behaviour of the company or organization behind the product is of no concern to the customer.

### 3.4.2  Optimization

In the second phase, product development is broadened to include ergonomic aspects and issues of reliability in use and safety. The 'optimization' product phase is characterized as follows. Although the product
is, technically speaking, still new, consumer awareness of the product is
starting to develop. The performance of the product is reasonable, but
product development is still aimed at improving performance. Other
aspects, such as increased reliability, improving ergonomics and safety
aspects are becoming serious considerations. The price per unit is still
relatively high, but increasing competition creates a tendency towards
lower prices. In this and the following phase it can be advantageous
to involve clients in the product development process to improve the
performance and ergonomics.

**Summary**
1. The product is new to the market or there is some consumer awareness. It often results from a 'technology' push.
2. The performance of the product is reasonable.
3. Product development is aimed at improving performance, better
   reliability, improvement of ergonomics and safety.
4. Form giving is not very important, and therefore matching form
   giving to different parts of the product is poor.
5. The price per unit can still be relatively high, although there is more
   competition.
6. The product is designed for production with standard machining,
   the product usually has many parts, and assembly is often done by
   hand.
7. There is no organized service organization.
8. The social behaviour of the company or organization behind the
   product is of no concern to the customer.

### 3.4.3  Itemization

When producers have improved their product to the point that they
satisfy generally accepted standards of functionality and reliability,
the edge of competition shifts to convenience. Buyers will prefer those
products that are the most convenient to use and – especially in the
business-to-business market – sellers that are convenient to deal with.
Mass-produced products make personal selling impossible. The market
grows less and the number of competitors increases. As the product
range grows, prices fall and promotion costs increase. Efforts are made
to develop extra features and accessories, including special editions of
the product that are developed for different trade channels and target
groups. Design becomes more important, and product aesthetics
becomes a major concern. The number of product parts of the basic
(cheapest) products decreases, but accessories or extra features can
cause an opposite effect, namely an increase in the number of parts.
Mechanic and/or automatic assembly also becomes more important. If
needed, well-organized service organizations are set up to support the
product.

**Summary**

1. There is some consumer awareness of the product.
2. The functionality and reliability of the product are good. The ergonomics and human interface are acceptable, and the product is safe.
3. Product development is still aimed at improving performance, reliability, ergonomics, human interfaces and safety. Efforts are made to develop extra features and accessories, including special editions of the product that are developed for different trade channels and target groups.
4. The matching of the form giving of different parts (integration of form giving) with the product is good.
5. Prices start falling.
6. The number of product parts (of the basic product) decreases, and automation becomes more important. However the development of extra features and accessories (see 3) can cause an opposite effect.
7. There is a well-organized service organization to support the product.
8. The social behaviour of the company or organization behind the product is of very little or no concern to the customer.

### 3.4.4 Segmentation, Individualization and Awareness

In the original study, based on five retrospective case studies and a classification by experts (Eger, 2007), it was proposed that the product phases follow one another. Based on additional studies, it can be concluded that the last three phases often exist simultaneously, and that one or two of these phases are sometimes not suitable for the product or product group. This summary examines all three product phases.

**Summary**

1. Almost all members of the target group know the product or have heard of it.
2. The functionality, reliability, ergonomics and human interface of the product are good and the product is safe. The customer therefore has plenty of choice thanks to the broad product range.
3. Product development is aimed at extra features and accessories, including special editions of the product for different trade channels and target groups.
4. The matching of the form giving of different parts (integration of form giving) with the product is good.
5. Since competitors' prices are low, it is almost impossible for a company to lower their prices even further.
6. The number of product parts decreases. Production and assembly are highly automated.
7. There is a well-organized 'service organization' to support the product.

### 3.4.5 Segmentation

In the first three product phases (i.e., performance, optimization and itemization) the focus was on improved functionality, reliability, ergonomics and safety. An attempt to add extra features and accessories in order to differentiate the product from its competitors takes place somewhere in the third stage. However, this kind of development comes to an end. Indeed, there comes a time when the performance offered is actually greater than the performance required. For relatively uncomplicated products, such as furniture and trinkets, the possibilities for adding features or accessories are limited. Moreover, products become less attractive to innovators and early adopters during the latter product phases. The market share is such that the product is considered to be 'accepted'. Owning the product is no longer distinctive, as it does not offer any form of status. Adding emotional benefits to a product is now possible. Recent research (Candi et al., 2010) has shown that involving customers in the design of emotional benefits (experience design) does not improve the success of the product.

Characteristics of the product phase 'segmentation' are that almost all members of the target group know the product from their own experience, or have at least heard of it. As the product, technically speaking, enters the domain of some 'dominant design' (or a limited number of 'dominant designs'), product development is aimed at adding extra features and accessories, including special editions of the product for different trade channels and target groups. Design has then reached a stage of complete integration of the different parts of the product into a completely unified and recognizable form, and the design focus shifts from form giving proper to expressive features, aimed at increasing emotional benefits. The market approaches perfect competition.

### Summary
(Only the product characteristics that are distinctive for this product phase are mentioned.)
4. Form giving becomes more expressive (styling) and is aimed at adding emotional benefits.
5. By adding emotional benefits the company can realize better prices.
8. The social behaviour of the company or organization behind the product is of little or no concern to the customer.

### 3.4.6 Individualization

Extrapolation of segmentation (continuous fine tuning of products on ever smaller target groups) ultimately leads to a product that is properly attuned to one individual. The developments in information and production technology make this kind of individualization even more possible. These developments imply the following changes in characteristics in the 'individualization' product phase. Product development is geared to mass customization and co-creation, allowing the customer to influence the final result. The market starts to shift from a homogeneous polypoly into a heterogeneous polypoly. Although prices approach average technical production costs of the dominant design, co-creation and mass customization offer possibilities to realize higher prices. Interactive media are used to customize the product to the needs of the individual customer.

**Summary**

(Only the product characteristics that are distinctive for this product phase are mentioned.)

3  Product development is aimed at mass customization or co-creation, allowing the customer to influence the final result.

4. Form giving becomes more expressive (styling) and is aimed at adding emotional benefits.

5. Co-creation and mass customization can offer possibilities for realizing higher prices. Interactive media are used to customize the product to meet the needs of the individual.

8. The social behaviour of the company or organization behind the product is becoming more and more important to the customer.

### 3.4.7  Awareness

A substantial proportion of consumers are willing to contribute to a better environment and to help in solving societal problems by changing their consumption patterns, but only if this can be done without much effort, and only if it does not lead to a decrease in consumer satisfaction and an increase in the financial burden. Most people expect companies to play an active role in solving common societal problems. A company can successfully tempt consumers – especially those who are committed to purchasing luxury products – by offering them the possibility of showing their ethical involvement by acquiring products that in some way claim to be more environmentally or socially beneficial than those of their competitors. This leads to slight changes in the characteristics of the last product phase, 'awareness'. The addition of extra features and accessories, including special editions of the product for different trade channels and target groups, has not stopped, but becomes a secondary concern. Design is focused on the enhancement of expressive features, aimed at increasing emotional benefits. However, when these benefits start to include ethical concerns, this can lead to a sudden leap into ascetic and sober forms. This tendency is reinforced even more by product claims on societal and environmental issues. The producing company explicitly communicates company ethics in its promotion campaigns. The ethical behaviour of the producing company does influence – to some extent – consumers' choices.

**Summary**

(Only the product characteristics that are distinctive for this product phase are mentioned.)

4. The matching of the form giving of different parts (integration of form giving) of the product is good, but in this phase that often means a rather sober design.

8. The social behaviour of the company or organization behind the product is a major concern to the customer. The organization communicates the ethics of the company concerning the society and the environment.

## 3.5  How to Use the Model

The phenomena that appear during the phases of the life of a product have been described. The regularities that were found have been analyzed and described. This has led to the six product phases: performance, optimization, itemization, segmentation, individualization, and awareness. The six phases are placed in chronological order in such a way that any predictions about new or future products can be made. This can be done by positioning a product, based on its product characteristics, in one of the product phases. When developing a future product, a designer can add to the product characteristics of (one of) the next product phase(s), thus creating added value for the intended user. In this way, the product phases can help a designer to create the next generation of a product.

Some remarks can be made regarding the theory of product phases (see also Chapter 7). The first phases have been defined with more accuracy than the latter. It seems that the 'career' of a product varies considerably as time progresses. Perhaps there is an analogy between the career of a human being and that of a product. It will be shown (see Chapter 5) that external factors can disturb the course of the product phases. It also appears that it is hard to draw a fine line between two different, successive product phases, as product phases can exist concurrently (see Chapters 4 and 7). Despite these limitations, the theory of product phases has proven to be a useful thinking aid in order to make the large variation in 'product careers' well-structured and unambiguous.

### 3.5.1  Education

With regard to schooling, the theory has proven to be a useful tool to teach students to incorporate the history of a product into their design process when developing a new product and to develop a next logical step instead of trying to make an 'innovative jump' (see Section 7.3). This is important as most of the products that are developed are very rarely 'completely new' (and sometimes 'not new at all'), since they are often the successors of existing products that have minimal differences from their predecessors.

### 3.5.2  Design Practice

In his design practice, a designer can use the product phases in order to guide the new product development. He can also use it as a means in the decision process. Designers seldom decide whether a product will be manufactured and introduced into the market, since this decision is usually made by the entrepreneur or manager in charge of the project (Forty, 1986). However, in most cases the designer has to convince his client. When doing so he can make use of the product phases to explain why and on what grounds certain decisions were made. Finally, a designer who has his own agency can use the product phases as an acquisition tool. If he studies the history of the products of his prospect he can give them (even in the first meeting) a vision on the main lines of his future product assortment.

**Implementation phase**
· Product documentation
· Product information
· Project evaluation
· Realization

**Embodiment and detailing phase**
· Detailing
· Calculation/simulation
· Prototype
· Prototype evaluation
· Design adaptations/ refinements

**Design phase**
· Concept phase
· Feasibility and planning
· Product definition
· Design
· Models
· Tests

**Preliminary phase**
· Kick-off meeting
· Market research
· Usability evaluation
· Design strategy
· Product analysis

In general it can be concluded that the theory offers a useful tool in the first steps of a new product development project: the Preliminary phase (Figure 3.5.1), where existing, competing products are studied with regard to their functionality, ergonomics, safety and marketing; and in the phase where ideas are generated for the preliminary design (Design phase, Figure 3.5.1). On the other hand, the theory does always offer several options, never only one; and these options are not very detailed, leaving a lot of room for the designer to choose and detail the chosen concept.

### 3.5.3  Styling

According to the theory, a new product starts in the performance phase and goes through the next phases to finally come into the last three phases: segmentation, individualization and awareness. The higher the product phase that is reached, the more important styling becomes. Up to the phase of itemization the styling should be rather neutral, not too expressive. However, in the phase of segmentation the styling will become more expressive, on the one hand to make the product attractive for the chosen target groups, and on the other hand to distinguish the product from the in this phase often wide range of offerings. In the awareness phase the behaviour of the producer or the brand will become more important. The price/performance ratio between products becomes so equal that the image of the brand starts to play a role in the buying decisions. What is the social behaviour of the company? What do they do to improve the environment? Etc. This may lead to a much less expressive, more sober styling of the products.

# 4 RETROSPECTIVE CASE SURVEYS

In this section the history of five products is analyzed in a comparative multiple retrospective case survey (see also Section 7.1). This consisted of a literature study and interviews with people involved in the products, such as directors, marketing managers, product managers and designers. The following products were analyzed: electric shavers (Section 4.1), mobile phones (4.2), bicycles (4.3), working-class housing (4.4) and travelling (4.5).

## 4.1 Electric Shaver

Until the beginning of the twentieth century, shaving was a task carried out by hairdressers. Only after the invention and introduction of disposable razor blades in 1903 did shaving slowly become an activity carried out in the home. Even though they were originally called 'safety razors', they still often caused cuts. The lack of safety and the fact that not every home was equipped with running water were the reasons to develop dry shaving. In 1929 Schick was the first company to introduce an electric dry shaver. In this section the development of electric shaving is described and analyzed on the basis of the Philips electric shavers. Philips was chosen because it is the leading manufacturer of electric shavers. Philips was one of the first producers of electric shavers and has been market leader for over 50 years (Baudet, 1986; Dijkstra, 2005; Marzano, 2005; Van Oost, 2003).

In 1937 Alexandre 'Sacha' Horowitz, head of Philips Laboratories for Appliances, was assigned the task of developing an electric shaver. Horowitz started by analyzing the electric shavers that were on the market at that time. The first dry shaver that Schick brought onto the market in 1929 was what was referred to as the vibration type, consisting of small knives that moved to and fro behind a grid. Ramakers (1984) wrote the following about these shavers. 'The skin was heavily irritated and the appliances continuously pulled out beard hairs'. It is quite clear that this typically fits into the performance phase.

In 1939 Philips introduced its first Philishave at the annual Spring Exhibition (Voorjaarsbeurs) in Utrecht (The Netherlands). This electric shaver performed much better than existing products because of a system that was unique at the time. The Philishave had a circular shaving head with slots that pointed inwards, behind which three bronze knives rotated and cut the hairs. The design of the first products was not very distinctive. The black, Bakelite housing was more or less in line with shaver construction up to then, being a cylinder shape with, at one end, a chromed steel shaving head with a diameter of 17 mm and the electrical cord at the other end. The shaver was soon nicknamed 'the cigar'. Between 1940 and 1955, product development focused mainly on improving performance (Figure 4.1.1). In 1940 the shaving result was improved with the introduction of a skin tensioner. Shortly after that the shaving speed was improved by increasing the number of knives from three to six and by replacing the bronze knives with steel ones that did not break as quickly. In 1946 a new appliance, with a larger shaving head and a stronger motor, was introduced under the name 'Steel Beard' (Staalbaard), but the product was still far from perfect. Shaving took about twenty minutes, and many people still experienced problems with an irritated skin.

FIGURE 4.1.1
The development of the
Philishave between 1939
and 1962.

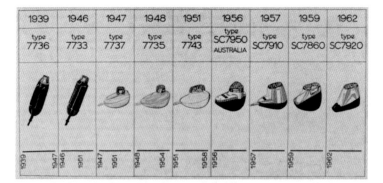

It took nearly 10 years, until after World War II, before more attention was paid to the styling of the Philishave. In 1947 a white, kind of egg-shaped shaver with the shaving head on one side was launched onto the market (see Figures 4.1.1 and 4.1.3). This appliance, which was developed for the US market where Philips owned the Norelco brand, was still made of Bakelite. Its successor was introduced just one year later. It had an ivory colour and was made using urea formaldehyde. Bakelite was considered old-fashioned by that time. These two shavers saw physical ergonomics starting to play a role for the first time.
The designers were instructed to develop a shaver that fitted exactly into the palm of the hand. The slogan used was 'As if your hand invented it'. Even though styling had now started to play a role, product improvements were still possible and necessary.

Around 1940 Philips started setting up a network of dealers to help sell its electric shavers. These dealers received sales instructions and organized demonstrations (Dijkstra, 2005). In 1951 both the speed of shaving and the quality of the result had been significantly improved through the introduction of a double shaving head with corrugated shaving slots. In 1956 a shaver with three shaving heads was introduced. However, this three-headed shaver was introduced only in Australia and New Zealand. For reasons that are not known it was decided to continue the development of the two-headed shaver. In 1957 this appliance was equipped with a so-called 'flip top' cleaning system. The shaving head can be removed to be cleaned by a simple push of a button. In 1959 another important improvement was introduced, namely spring-driven shaving heads, which followed the contours of the face better and were even larger (22 mm) (Ramakers, 1984; Van Oost, 2003).

These improvements marked the beginning of the optimization phase. It would take until 1966 before Philips introduced the three-headed shaver worldwide, which had been tested 10 years earlier. After some styling and colour adjustments in 1975, Philips again introduced a complete redesign: the so-called TH-design (telephone head). The shaver could stand (see Figure 4.1.2), and the shaving heads were positioned at an angle of 90°. After 1975 the light colour and rounded forms of the Philishave disappeared. Instead, the colours become metallic in combination with black. The product styling became more angular. Another important improvement was introduced in 1980 in the form of a 'double action' system. The system was equipped with two knives that were placed in close proximity to each other. The idea was that the first knife would lift the hair a little, after which the second knife cut it off. The goal was, of course, a better shaving result. Real innovations and improvements then became rarer, and the time between the introductions increased. Although Philips had already introduced a battery-operated two-headed shaver in 1952 and one with rechargeable batteries in 1966, it would take until the 1980s before shavers with rechargeable batteries became a success. This was because it was only then that the technique was advanced enough to make it possible (Figure 4.1.6). During the same decade the shavers were equipped with displays showing information on the amount of energy left in the battery and the amount of time the shaver could still be used. Most of these features can be considered 'extras' and therefore belong in the itemization product phase. In 1998 Philips introduced the 'Cool Skin', a shaver that applied an emulsion to the skin during shaving. This caused a sensation reminiscent of wet shaving. The shaver was particularly successful in the USA, where, up to then, around 75% of men still shaved wet.

The promotional activities changed between 1950 and 1970 from the giving of personal information and demonstrations to the involvement of celebrities. The two-headed shaver can be seen in the movie 'The Long Wait', and commercials were made with Buster Keaton.

The introduction of the first shaver in 1939 showed that Philips had already realized that women were an interesting target group for their products that, at the time, were solely aimed at men. The manual included a short explanation for women. However, it would take until 1951 before a shaver for women appeared on the market. It was called 'The Beautiphil'. The technical differences from the Philishave were small. The slots in the shaving head were somewhat wider, and the space in which shaved hair was (temporarily) stored was a little larger.

The most important difference was in the packaging of the ladies' shaver (see Figures 4.1.3 and 4.1.4).

It would take until 1959 before Philips introduced a special design for women, which was known as 'The Lipstick' (Figure 4.1.5). In its design a clear link is made to cosmetics. Contrary to what had been done with regard to the styling of the men's shaver, the technical elements were hidden wherever possible. Some of the measures were quite extreme. For example, the product even had a small cushion with perfume to suppress the smell of the oil in the device. In 1960 Philips changed to a vibrating system for ladies' shavers (the system used by their competitors, Braun and Remington). In 1967 production moved to Klagenfurt (in Austria). It was at around that time that segmentation really started. The styling of the machines for men became more angular and the shavers were available in different colours. The ladies' shavers became more cosmetic. While the technological features were emphasized in the men's shavers, in the ladies' shavers such features were hidden wherever possible.

The segmentation phase has now been reached. Nearly everybody knew what an electric shaver did and how well it functioned. The manufacturers tried to reach different target groups and lifestyles using styling. Braun introduced a shaver in which a lot of attention had been paid to the tactile experience. Black, plastic bumps stick through a metallic housing, which gives a pleasant feeling in the hand (Figure 4.1.6). Since 1985 Philips has also focused on young men, for instance in the form of the Tracer. An important reason for doing this was that research has shown that men who start using an electric shaver are most likely to continue doing so for the rest of their lives. In this phase nearly all electric shavers had rechargeable batteries, meaning that the user does not have to have an electric socket close to hand.

Advertising activities were becoming more common. Besides commercials on radio, television and in magazines, sportsmen were also sponsored by Philips. In the movie *Die Another Day* (2002) James Bond uses a Philishave. Philips' intention is clear. The expectation was that using famous sportsmen and movie stars would cause consumers to identify with them and therefore choose the Philips brand.

In 2003, 60 products were on display on the Philips website (Personal Care). Half of them related to electric shavers: Cool Skin (6 different devices), Sensotec (7) (Figure 4.1.7), Super Reflex (4), Quadro Action (6), Micro+ (3), Turbo Vac (2) and 2 beard trimmers. The other half consisted of components such as shaving heads, or accessories such as cleaning sets or gel (for the Cool Skin shavers).

It is difficult to realize an individualization product phase for electric shavers. For example, a mobile phone (see Section 4.2) is something people carry on their person, and it therefore has a significant 'expression value' (anyone can see it, or you can show it to anyone). However, the electric shaver remains (and has remained) a bathroom product.

FIGURE 4.1.3
The egg-shaped device made by
Philips (1948); the version for men.

FIGURE 4.1.4
The egg-shaped device made by
Philips (1951); the version for women.

FIGURE 4.1.5
'Lipstick', the first Philips
shaver designed specially
for women (1959).

FIGURE 4.1.6
An electric shaver from Braun, in
which special attention was paid
to tactile aspects. The shaver was
equipped with rechargeable
batteries for wireless shaving
(around 1980).

FIGURE 4.1.7
Philips Sensotec, available in
several colours, with rechargeable
batteries for wireless shaving
(2003 range).

Although it is technically feasible to mould a shaver to a customer's hand in a shop, such service is not yet expected.

The product phase awareness has, however, been more or less realized by manufacturers in the past. An example is an action of Braun at the end of the twentieth century, where used shavers were taken back. These kinds of activities not only offer users an extra discount, they also solve the problem they have with throwing away a product that still functions perfectly well. In the process it is important that the company makes it clear that the collected shavers are dealt with in a responsible way (e.g. by recycling). For years Philips has been active in profiling itself as a responsible company. According to the Dow Jones Sustainability Index, Philips was market leader with regard to environmentally responsible entrepreneurship in both 2004 and in 2005.

### Summary

This section analyzed and described shavers on the basis of the Philips products. Philips was chosen because it has been a market leader in shavers for over 40 years. The development of the (Philips) shaver follows the theory very closely. With regard to the first two phases, some information is missing concerning pricing, production, service and ethics. During the individualization and awareness part of the product phases only some of the product characteristics are partially fulfilled. With regard to 'product development' this means that new product development is aimed at different target groups, but not at individuals. As far as 'pricing' is concerned, this means that there is a lot of competition on the basis of product price. However, this does not mean that the price can be increased because the product has been customized.

## 4.2 Mobile Phone

The mobile phone has a short history compared with the electric shaver. The concept was developed in 1947 by Bell Laboratories under the supervision of Dr Martin Cooper (Anonymous, 2004, 2005a). However, the development was not continued because, at that time, the Federal Communications Committee (FCC) made so little frequencies available that only a maximum of 23 phone calls would be possible simultaneously per service area. In short, the FCC did not believe in the possibilities of mobile phones. It would take until 1968 before the FCC reconsidered its decision and was prepared to increase the number of frequencies, subject to technological improvements.

FIGURE 4.2.1
Motorola DynaTAC 8000X, the first commercially available mobile phone.

It would take until 6 March 1983 before the mobile phone was introduced commercially. In that year the Motorola DynaTAC 8000X (Figure 4.2.1) was to be the first 'FCC-approved portable cellular phone'. Until then Motorola had worked for 15 years on the project and spent $100 million. The DynaTAC (DynaTAC stands for Dynamic Adaptive Total Area Coverage) weighed nearly 1 kg (870 g to be precise), measured 33 × 9 × 4.5 cm and had a LED display. It could be used to make phone calls for up to one hour, and its standby time was eight hours. It took 10 hours to recharge the batteries. The phone had a memory that could store 30 phone numbers. Despite the price of $3,995.00 there was a waiting list, shortly after its introduction, of many thousands of consumers who wanted to buy the product. The phone had very limited options. The necessary infrastructure was far from ready. So there were only a few places from where it could be used. It is quite clear that the first products fulfilled the criteria of the product phase performance. Rudy Krolopp (Figure 4.2.2), one of the members of the team that developed the Motorola DynaTAC, said the following:

FIGURE 4.2.2
Rudy Krolopp, member of the design team that developed the DynaTAC 8000X.

In 1983, the notion of simply making wireless phone calls was revolutionary and it was an exciting time to be pioneering the technology at Motorola. Marty (Dr Martin Cooper) called me into his office one day in December 1972 and said 'We've got to build a portable cell phone' and I said 'What the hell's a portable cell phone?  *(Anonymous, 2005a, p. 2)*

Until the beginning of the 1990s the developments with regard to mobile phones focused on product improvement. Special attention was paid to reliability, weight reduction, miniaturization and completing the infrastructure. The developments took place in rapid succession (Figure 4.2.3). In 1992, for example, Nokia introduced its 1011. The device weighed 470 g and measured 19.5 × 6 × 4.5 cm (Figure 4.2.4). In that same year Ericsson introduced the GH198, which weighed 330 g and measured 14.7 × 6.6 × 3.1 cm (Figure 4.2.5).

FIGURE 4.2.3
Growth (worldwide) of the number of mobile phones compared with the number of fixed lines.

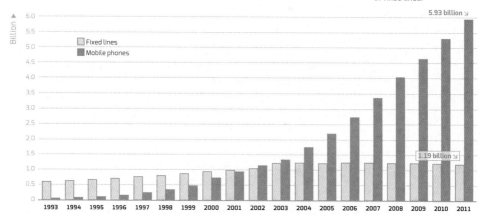

The first really handy mobile phones appeared on the market in the mid-1990s. In 1994 Nokia introduced the 2100 series. In a few years 20 million of the mobiles were sold worldwide (Anonymous, 2005b). In 1995 Ericsson introduced the NH237 (at the moment of introduction it was the smallest mobile in the world). This phone remained on the market until 1997. Figure 4.2.6 shows the next generation of this phone. With regard to its neutral styling, this product is identical to its predecessor. By now mobile phones weighed about 200 g and measured about 15 × 6 × 2 cm.

In an article in *Design Engineering* (Anonymous, 1997) it was concluded that competition between manufacturers is based mainly on price, size and lifetime of the battery.

Manufacturers of modern digital cellular telephones compete principally on the basis of price, size and battery lifetime. [...] Typically, an existing amplifier in a digital cellular telephone is 35% efficient, with 65% of the power wasted as heat. This gives a typical talk time between battery charges of 2hr.   *(Anonymous, 1997, p. 11)*

In a later study (Karjaluoto, 2005) a change in these criteria is found that suits the product phase segmentation. According to this research amongst students in Finland, the most important criteria are price, brand, user interface and (technical) features. The design, which is the styling of the phone, also plays a – less important – role.

The product phases follow one another in a short period. This can be explained by the rapid acceptance of the product. The reason for this is most likely that the product is in fact not really new. It can be regarded as an important improvement of an existing product, namely a telephone that is not mobile because it is wired. As early as in 1996, mobiles were launched onto the market with characteristics of the segmentation phase. For example, Ericsson introduced the GH388, which was aimed at the Business to Business market. A comparable product that was aimed at the consumer market was available in three colours, namely green, blue and grey. This phone was the one on which the GF388 was based. It has a flap that covers the buttons. Separate flaps were introduced as accessories with prints by famous artists, such as Keith Haring, Roy Lichtenstein, Chagall, Picasso and (see Figure 4.2.7) Moholy-Nagy.

In her paper, Srivastava (2005) provides some interesting examples of segmentation. For example, LG Electronics introduced a telephone with a built-in compass onto the market. This feature allowed Muslims to find Mecca for their obligatory prayers five times a day.

A mobile phone became a status symbol, especially for young people.

A lot of young people show off their mobile phones to each other. The ringtones they use and the number and quality of messages stored on their mobile phones enhances their social status. [...] In Japan, mobile users personalize their mobile phone with stickers and colourful beaded accessories. Fashionable wallpaper can be downloaded to enhance the look of the mobile. If that's not enough, 'designer mobiles' have appeared on the market, with everything from embedded precious stones to leather or fur covers for every occasion and mood. *(Srivastava, 2005, p. 115)*

Young people use the mobile primarily to sustain and enhance their social networks. It allows them to maintain their status, in terms of age, gender, class, peer group and so on.   *(Srivastava, 2005, p. 121)*

FIGURE 4.2.4
Nokia 1011, introduction 1992, measured: 19.5 × 6 × 4.5 cm.

FIGURE 4.2.5
Ericsson GH198 (right), introduction 1992, measured: 14.7 × 6.6 × 3.1 cm, next to it (left) a more recent Nokia.

FIGURE 4.2.6
Ericsson NH238, weight: 234 g, measures: 13 × 4.0 × 2.2 cm (1994).

FIGURE 4.2.7
Ericsson GF388, with exchangeable flaps, in this example with works of Moholy-Nagy (1995).

FIGURE 4.2.8
Vertu, 18 carat gold, with butler button, €14,000 (2002).

FIGURE 4.2.9
The Lady Phone of Samsung (2003).

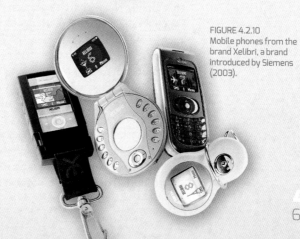

FIGURE 4.2.10
Mobile phones from the brand Xelibri, a brand introduced by Siemens (2003).

In 1999 the segmentation phase had clearly been reached. Ericsson, for example, introduced the A1018s series in three basic configurations, each with several variations:
- the A1018s Art, with six exchangeable design flaps,
- the A1018s TwinColour, with canvas belt holster and two exchangeable flaps,
- the A1018s Business, wine red, with portable hands free.

At the end of the 1990s, developments took place extremely quickly. Brands such as Nokia introduced over 12 new models each year. In 2002 Samsung launched the Lady Phone (Figure 4.2.9). This red mobile phone with a consumer price of €499.00 has a clock on the front that is surrounded by fake little diamonds. These light up in different colours so that the owner can see who is calling. Furthermore, the Lady Phone has a mirror and a menstruation calendar to predict the owner's fertile days. In 2004 the Lady Phone was also introduced in blue, white and gold. Figure 4.2.10 shows some phones of the Xelibri brand (Siemens). By now a lot of mobiles were available with downloaded graphic symbols, ringtones, etc (individualization).

FIGURE 4.2.11
De Volkskrant: 'Promotional photo for the Alcatel One Touch. Brands put more emphasis on emotional benefits since their technique is no longer unique' (2005).

In a study on the social consequences of the introduction of the mobile phone by Srivastava (2005), it was concluded that the design and use of mobile phones have huge consequences for the individuality of the users.

FIGURE 4.2.12
Market stall with accessories to individualize the mobile phone on the market Van Heekplein in Enschede, the Netherlands (2005).

[…] The highly personalized nature of the mobile phone has meant that its form and use have become important aspects of the individuality of a phone user. Banking on this trend, many manufacturers are embedding the latest fashion trends into their mobile handsets, and providing a wide array of services for users, personalizing their phones (e.g. mobile wallpaper, ring tones, coloured phone covers, etcetera).
(Srivastava, 2005, p. 112)

Moreover, the extent and nature of the personalization of the telephone is now essential to individual identity, particularly among the youth.
(Srivastava, 2005, p. 115)

An article in the Dutch newspaper De Volkskrant (Didde, 2004) shows that mobile phones have also reached the awareness phase. The article describes the collecting of used mobiles by the company Recell. For each mobile phone that is collected, Recell donates a sum of money to a charity. In 2003 Recell collected over 35,000 mobiles. Considering the number of unused mobile phones, this number is not that high. According to the same article, 14 million mobiles were in use in the Netherlands in 2004, while another 15 million were lying unused in drawers or cupboards. Recell repaired the collected mobiles (if necessary) and then exported them to countries in Africa or Asia. The company recognized that they were also exporting a waste problem. They tried to organize a collecting structure in the countries to which they exported the products, but that produced almost no response.

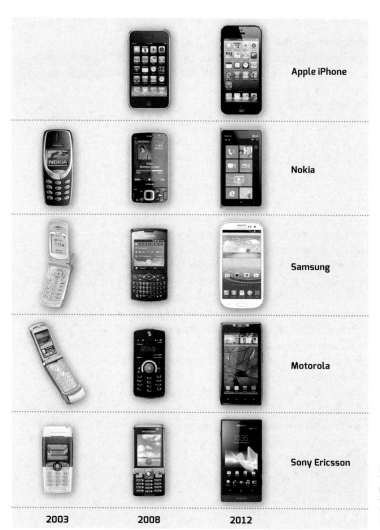

FIGURE 4.2.13
The introduction of the iPhone seems to have led to a new dominant design for mobile phones (smartphones).

## A New Dominant Design

An interesting recent development is the appearance of a new dominant design, with Apple's introduction of the iPhone. While, until 2008, the focus of different mobile phone brands was on emphasizing the differences between the mobile phones (segmentation), the phones which came after this introduction – now called smartphones – started to look more alike (itemization, see also Figure 4.2.13). A new dominant design appeared. In order to distinguish between the brands one has to look at the user interface.

## Summary

In a short period of time the mobile phone passed through all the product phases and fulfilled almost all the product characteristics (Anonymous, 2004, 2005a, 2005b; Karjaluoto, 2005; Srivastava, 2005). Because of the quick development of the market and the enormous number of products sold in a short period of time, the mobile phone does not meet the product characteristics for 'production' in the product optimization phase. In addition, the product characteristic of 'number of competitors' is not met during the product segmentation phase. The description suggests that there are a lot of competitors, but, in reality, there are only a few large manufacturers. In the third quarter of 2005 the market shares were Nokia 33.2%, Motorola 18.5%, Samsung 13.4%, LG 6.6% and Sony Ericsson 6.5%.

## 4.3 Bicycle[4]

The bicycle largely follows the theory of product phases (Baudet, 1986; Bijker, 1990; Rietveld and Kuner, 1999; Van der Wal, 2005). In 1839 Kirkpatrick MacMillan designed the first bicycle with a system of pedals and bars used to drive the rear wheel. The Frenchman Michaud was the first to fix the pedals directly to the front wheel. His first bicycles were made of wood. In 1866, however, he started marketing a bicycle that was made completely of steel, and that, after an exhibition in Paris in 1869, became quite a success. Michaud bicycles were not at all comfortable to ride and required a lot of strength and skill. In the case of the first bicycles, participation in exhibitions, as Michaud experienced in Paris, and free publicity were the most important promotional activities. The pioneers of the bicycle attracted so much attention by simply riding their own bicycles in public that publications in papers and magazines followed 'of their own accord'. In 1871 James Starley introduced his 'Ariel', a bicycle that would become very success-ful under the names 'high bi' (Figure 4.3.1) and 'ordinary'. The 'Ariel' was the first bicycle with spokes. It had solid rubber tyres, a front wheel with a diameter of 125 cm and a rear wheel of 35 cm. In the beginning, the bicycle was mainly a product for the upper class and higher middle class youngsters, and was used for sports (competitions) and tourism. Riding a tall bicycle was quite dangerous since the centre of gravity is also quite high, near the axle of the big front wheel, meaning that there is a considerable risk of toppling over. Moreover, in the course of time the front wheel was made even bigger to allow faster cycling, and that further increased the risk.

In order to enlarge the market, a lot of manufacturers tried to solve the problem of toppling over that plagued the high bi. One of the earliest solutions designers sought – and found – was to build cycles with three or four wheels. Evidence that these efforts were indeed to some extent successful was provided by the Stanley Show in 1883, where 289 tricycles were displayed as opposed to 233 bicycles. Another solution involved moving the saddle towards the rear wheel. This led to two very success-ful cycles, namely the 'Facile' by Ellis & Co (1874) and the 'Xtraordinary' by Singer (1878). Another design strategy in those days entailed the development of totally new cycles that were driven by the rear wheel and whose saddle was close to the rear axle. Well-known examples are the American 'Star' (1881) with a small wheel at the front and a bigger one behind, and Lawson's 'Bicyclette' (1879) (Figure 4.3.2). The latter was

4   This case has been published before in *Design Issues* (Eger and Drukker, 2010).

FIGURE 4.3.1
A so-called 'high bi' from 1875.

FIGURE 4.3.2
Lawson's'
Bicyclette'
(1879).

FIGURE 4.3.3
'Rover Safety
Bicycle' (1885).

FIGURE 4.3.4
Moulton bike (1962).

FIGURE 4.3.5
Huffy вмх bike (1971).

FIGURE 4.3.6
Lawwill Pro Cruiser
All Terrain Bike (1980).

the first bicycle driven by a chain on the back wheel. In 1885 John Starley introduced the 'Rover Safety Bicycle' (Figure 4.3.3), generally considered to be the last step in the bicycle's evolution into the ones we know today.

In the 'performance' product phase, bicycles were exclusively used for sports and tourism. In the later phases, the transportation function slowly became important. Bicycles enabled people to move to cheaper houses, further away from their work.

Another important development relating to the bicycle was the invention of the pneumatic tyre in 1888 by John Boyd Dunlop. In 1890 about 98% of all tyres were solid, while six years later, in 1894, the market share of pneumatic tyres had grown to nearly 90%. According to Baudet, it was then that the bicycle reached its final stage. Up until the early 1990s, technical improvements (tyres, bearings, transmission, steering, etc.) had been quite important, sometimes even of fundamental interest. The bicycle, as we know it now, acquired its form in around 1895. Fundamental technological innovations, like those in the early stages of development, were not realized after that. The fact that the dominant design of the bicycle was realized around the end of the nineteenth century does not imply that it was completely impossible to make additional technical improvements on the bicycle after that time.

Van der Wal mentions:
- The development of the aluminium bicycle by the Frenchman Rupalley (1895).
- The introduction of the three-speed hub gear by Sturmey & Archer (1902).
- The invention of the derailleur in the 1930s, which became a success only after World War II.
- The introduction of the drum brake (1937).
- The development of synchronously operating brakes (1960).

However, during the first half of the twentieth century, the basic design of the bicycle remained unchanged. Men's bicycles had a 'diamond frame', while women's bicycles had a so-called 'lady's curve' because of the long skirts they wore. These days such bicycles are referred to as the 'grandma bike' ('omafiets'). Virtually all bicycles were black. It was not until after World War II that new models were introduced owing to the increasing competition of the new motorized bicycle (moped). These were called 'sports bicycles'. These cycles did not look like the present sport bikes at all. However, compared with other bicycles of the time, they looked quite dynamic, with smaller wheels (66 cm instead of 71 cm), a shorter wheelbase and narrow tyres. They were fitted with colour striping and chromium parts and could be equipped with many accessories such as decorated gear cases, white grips, special rear lights, saddles and handle bars, etc. From the 1920s onwards production of bicycles became increasingly mechanized. Manufacturers invested in automated lathes and specialized production halls with functional layouts. Despite that, a lot of assembly tasks still had to be performed by hand.

The 1960s marked another period of change in bicycle design, exemplified by the introduction of the 'Moulton bike' (1962), a folding bike with aluminium parts designed by Alexander Moulton (Figure 4.3.4), and the BMX (1971), developed in Los Angeles (Figure 4.3.5). The latter developed into the now well-known mountain bike or 'ATB' ('All Terrain Bike') in California in 1976 (Figure 4.3.6 shows an example from 1980). These developments mark the transition from the 'itemization' phase to the 'segmentation phase'. The 1980s saw the introduction of special bicycles for nearly any purpose: ATBs, shopping bicycles, children's bikes, recumbent bicycles, racing bikes, touring bikes, folding bikes, etc. New materials and production methods gave designers more freedom to vary the design of frame constructions. In this way, the bicycle slowly turned from being a mere means of transportation into a fashion and lifestyle product.

Around 1890 the price of an average bicycle in the Netherlands was the same as several months' (3-6) wages of an average workman. Despite the rising price level during the first decennia of the twentieth century, bicycle prices fell dramatically. Around 1935 they reached a minimum in absolute terms. At that time the nominal price of a bike was approximately 14% of its price in 1890. In real terms this is about 10% of its price in 1890. After the mid-1930s, prices started to rise again, until an average quality bicycle in 1970 cost (in nominal terms) the same as in 1890. This still means that, in real terms (that is, correcting for changes in the general price level), its price in 1970 was 15% of its 1890 price. In other words, in 1890 an average Dutch worker had to work for between three and six months to raise the money for a bicycle. In 1935 this had dropped to one month, and in 1965 to half a month. Between 1960 and 1970 segmentation meant that bicycle prices varied between €90 and far above €500 (a range of 1.39 times the average). Since then the price range of bicycles has increased even more.

Owing to their basic design (a frame to which all other parts and accessories are attached), the bicycle reached the individualization phase soon after its segmentation phase. The typical layout made it very easy to create variety with parts, and to remove, add, or change accessories, thereby individualizing the bicycle. Since about 1985 completely custom-made bicycles were widely available. Bicycles entered the awareness phase around 1980, but for reasons that are slightly different from what the theory of product phases predicts. During this period, the bicycle was rediscovered as a healthy and environmentally friendly alternative to the 'unhealthy and polluting' car. However, these qualities were not deliberately developed by manufacturers, for instance by using environmentally friendly materials and production processes, or by committing themselves to social responsibility. These qualities were simply inherent in the product itself since its inception and would have come to the surface anyway, even if manufacturers had had no environmental conscience at all.

## Summary
The bicycle follows the theory of product phases to a great extent. The first three phases are completed in accordance with the theory. Despite that, the history of the bicycle is, at some points, at odds with

the theory. This can partly be explained by its long and special history. Of course, the development of the bicycle was influenced by historical developments. However, in this case the statement could also be applied in reverse in some respects. The process of suburbanization became possible by, among other things, the bicycle (and later, to a greater extent, also by the introduction of the car). Thanks to the bicycle people were able to live farther away from their work. Some other interference with the theory can be attributed to the lack of materials caused by the Second World War, and to the introduction of the car and the moped.

## 4.4  Working-Class Housing[5]

This section describes a retrospective case survey of working-class housing in the UK, Belgium ('Sociale woningbouw') and the Netherlands ('Volkshuisvesting'). The UK was chosen because the problem – housing large numbers of people who came to the cities after the industrial revolution – started there. Belgium was chosen because Richard Foqué lives there, and the Netherlands was chosen because the author lives there, which means that the information was easy to access. The assumption is that the history in other countries will not differ much, but this has not been verified.

One of the conditions of the theory of product phases is that there is competition. Before the Public Health Act of 1848, working-class housing was left to the free market, in line with the doctrine of laissez-faire. Tarn (1973) describes the situation in the cities in England as follows.

England led the industrial revolution, its towns were larger and uglier than those of any other country, they were filled with great mills and factories belching forth acrid smoke and fumes. [...] Now, for the first time, they constituted a separate recognizable and articulate class, living together in well defined ghettos either newly run up by speculative builders around the gates of the works, or in old courts taken over and over-occupied [...] to leave the town was like escaping from hell itself. *(Tarn, 1973, p. xiii)*

By the middle of the century towns were places of poverty, ill health, disease, inadequate water supplies, non-existent drainage and garbage collection. The severity of the situation is reflected in an official account by a city missionary.

On my district is a house containing eight rooms [...] the parlour measures 18 ft. by 10 ft. [...] in this one room slept, on the night previous to my enquiry, 27 male and female adults, 31 children, and two or three dogs, making in all 58 human beings breathing the contaminated atmosphere of a close room.   *(Hansard, 1851)*

5   This case has been published before in 'Bringing the World into Culture' a 'Liber Amicorum' for Richard Foqué (Eger, 2009). This explains the chosen countries.

The large number of houses that was built in England in this period resulted from speculative developments that were, in most cases, totally uncontrolled. Before 1850, there were a few examples of public concern, financed from philanthropy and often fostered by a sense of guilt. An example was the Bagnigge Wells estate, built by the Society for Improving the Conditions of the Labouring Classes (SICLC) (Figure 4.4.1).

The history of public housing (Volkshuisvesting) in Belgium started halfway through the nineteenth century. Cities were growing rapidly owing to the Industrial Revolution. The number of inhabitants of Brussels (and its environs) grew from 260,000 in 1850 to 760,000 in 1900 (De Pauw, 2006). The consequence was an enormous housing shortage. In 1868 a group of private persons started a charitable organization – the Société Anonyme des Habitants Ouvrières dans l'Agglomération Bruxelloise – that built working-class housing in Sint-Gillis, Anderlecht, Vorst, Molenbeek, and Schaarbeek (Figure 4.4.2). The first Public Housing Act was passed in 1889. This law made it possible to borrow money at a low rate of interest and led to the construction of 60,000 quite basic homes in Belgium between 1890 and 1914.

In the Netherlands public housing started to be developed after the passing of the Housing Act (Woningwet) of 1901. This Act was a response to the miserable situation in working-class areas at the end of the nineteenth century (Anonymous, 2001). The Act was motivated primarily by public hygiene issues. At first only small changes were made in the new houses. Rooms without fresh air, such as alcoves and box beds, were no longer permitted. In the first few years after the Act had been passed, only a small number of houses were built. Whether it was possible to build often depended on the personal efforts of civil servants or statesmen. The houses were sober and traditional in appearance. The fact that product performance was often poor and prices were relatively high meant that working-class housing followed the product phases theory. One can even say that it resulted from a 'technology push', although this did not come from the building industry, but from the industrial revolution itself. The demand for housing was so high that any square metre could be used and the people renting them could be (and were) exploited.

On 30 March 1847, Lord Morpeth introduced the first version of the Public Health Act in the UK. The Bill had clearly been prepared in haste and had a rough passage. The government withdrew it on 8 July. On 10 February the following year, Morpeth introduced a revised Bill that was intended to have – amongst others – the following effect: to make public sewers, to require owners or occupiers to provide house drains, to cleanse streets, to cleanse, cover or fill up offensive ditches, to provide sufficient supply of water, to alter drains, privies, water closets, and cesspools built contrary to the Act, to make bye-laws with respect to the removal of filth, and the emptying of privies. The battle for the passage of this Bill was as great as in the previous year. During the debate, the following, rather shocking, passage appeared in *The Economist*.

In our condition, suffering and evil are nature's admonitions; they cannot be got rid of; and the impatient attempts of benevolence to banish them from the world by legislation, before benevolence has learned their object and their end, have always been more productive of more evil than good. *(The Economist, 1848)*

Although the Bill was passed, it should be emphasized that the degree of success was minor. Until 1875, most buildings for working-class housing that were 'better' in the sense that they were well built had good ventilation, drainage, and an ample supply of water and had sometimes been designed by an architect, were (personal) charity initiatives, or initiatives by organizations like the SICLC. However, in 1890, Tarn (1973) speaks of houses with a

variety of types and standards of accommodation […] on the ground floor were shops with living accommodation arranged in the rear around small yards. *(Tarn, 1973, p. 101)*

The buildings became more visually attractive and there were experiments with the façades. For instance, cast iron balconies were constructed to avoid the monotonous regularity of the barrack-like buildings of earlier decades. After 1905, some architects adopted a modified classic style in an attempt to get away from the rather ponderous and oppressive quality of the earlier housing blocks.

The 1920s were the most important years for working-class housing in Belgium. In this period, garden quarters were built, such as Logis-Floréal in Watermaal-Bosvoorde (Figure 4.4.3), Cité Moderne in St. Agatha Berchem, and Kapelleveld in St. Lambrechts Woluwe. However, cheap, compact buildings were also built in city centres. From 1926 onwards the rate of building slowed because the construction of garden quarters was considered to be too expensive, and to take up too much space. Another reason was that the liberal government wanted to promote private ownership of houses (De Pauw, 2006).

In the Netherlands housing construction stopped almost completely during the First World War. When the construction of buildings restarted, the government exerted a lot of influence. Typical projects were large-scale building blocks. Examples are the Berlage buildings in Amsterdam, Van Elmpt in Groningen and the first Amsterdam School buildings (Figure 4.4.4). The most important aspect was not the floor plan, but the façade and the way it matched its surroundings. During the depression, the number of projects decreased, but two important developments started, namely row-building and multi-storey building. Although both developments were continued after the war, the poor quality of these buildings meant that many were demolished or thoroughly renovated.

It would appear that a 'dominant design' became discernible in England at the beginning of the twentieth century, namely a cottage with two levels, three bedrooms and, in the case of the larger types, a bathroom.

FIGURE 4.4.1
The Bagnigge Wells estate, the
first development of the SICLC.
Architect: Henry Roberts.

FIGURE 4.4.2
Linthoutwijk, Schaarbeek
(1870).

FIGURE 4.4.3
Floréal, Watermaal-
Bosvoorde.

FIGURE 4.4.4
'Het Schip', Spaarndammer-
buurt, Amsterdam.
Architect: M. de Klerk.

FIGURE 4.4.5
Spherical houses
('Bolwoningen') built
in 's Hertogenbosch in
1985. Architect: Dries
Kreijkamp.

FIGURE 4.4.7a
Two (originally identical) housing blocks in Enschede ...

FIGURE 4.4.7b
... and what people did to individualize them.

Development continued until 1911, but latterly the demand was for smaller houses for rents which the poorest class could afford, since private enterprise catered very adequately for the artisan who could afford a normal house with three bedrooms. *(Tarn, 1973, p. 138)*

In the Netherlands of the 1950s the emphasis was increasingly put on building quickly and cheaply, as well as building as many houses as possible. The key words were 'increase in scale' and 'standardization'. Complete residential neighbourhoods were set up, including playgrounds and parks for recreation. This tendency continued in the 1960s. In this period, large-scale projects such as the Bijlmermeer (Amsterdam) and Hoog-Catharijne (Utrecht) were developed (Anonymous, 2001). The result was uniformity. Architects started to break with this trend by trying to create – within the limits stipulated by the Dutch rules – variations by designing unusual housing types, by creating public gardens and by adjusting the plan of the area to the existing situation.

Even in 1885 there is some awareness of segmentation. Tarn (1973) mentions a publication that says: we must take the working class as consisting of various degrees; the upper, middle and lower of the labouring classes. In the 1970s, the attention 'on the continent' shifted to more attention on the individual. The development projects became smaller. The Dutch government made funds available for experimental building. In the field of public housing, experiments were carried out with the design and use of materials. Examples are Kasbah (in Hengelo) and the Bolwoningen (in 's Hertogenbosch) (Figure 4.4.5). Suitable housing was developed for elderly people, for singles and for small families. In Belgium the quantity of working-class housing seems to have remained low, although it is difficult to find detailed information (De Meyer and Smets, 1982) (Figure 4.4.6).

FIGURE 4.4.6
The number of private houses compared with the number of public houses built in Brussels between 1989 and 2004.

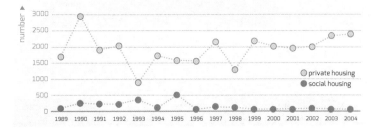

At the end of the nineteenth century, the first signs of individualization can already be perceived.

The identity of the individual had been lost in a Georgian terrace behind reticent, similar façades, designed to produce a harmonious street or square, rather than to glorify the separateness of each house. The rising class who possessed the money to own and build such houses were now no longer content with this reticence; they required that their social advancement should be more ostentatiously paraded by a showy individualistic house. *(Tarn, 1973, p. 153)*

FIGURE 4.4.8
Example of 'Het Wilde
Bouwen' in Roombeek,
Enschede.

In the 1980s and 1990s, more attention was paid to architecture in the Netherlands. The consequences of the energy crisis of the 1970s had an effect on building projects. In many projects, both private and social housing was built to create a good social mix of residents. The rising costs of the social tenement houses was compensated for by the benefits of the private housing. A new development was the building of shells that enable the inhabitants to influence the plan of their future home. It looks like there was almost a century between individualization in England and that in the Netherlands. Figure 4.4.7 shows very clearly the wish to individualize one's home.

In recent years 'random building' ('Het Wilde Bouwen') was introduced in the Netherlands. 'Anything goes' in certain areas, as long as people stick to the legal regulations concerning construction, ventilation, insulation, etc. Roombeek (in Enschede) is an example of such an area (Figure 4.4.8).

As already mentioned, the energy crises led to renewed house building, for example due to insulation and other energy saving measures.

In the last decade of the twentieth century, special 'green building' quarters ('Milieuwijken') were developed in the Netherlands. Examples are the Ecowijk in the Westerpark district of Amsterdam (Figure 4.4.9) and Oikos in Enschede.

FIGURE 4.4.9
The 'green building' quarter
Westerpark in Amsterdam.
Urban architect: Kees
Christiaans.

## Summary

The market for private and social housing is different in several ways from the market of products. First of all, there is the location of the house. This is an aspect that is not relevant to products, but is very important for houses. It means, for instance, that people sometimes do not have much choice unless they are willing to accept travelling long distances to and from their work. In addition, there are more govern-mental rules and regulations for housing than for most other products. Finally, it is easy to individualize a house, usually easier than to indi-vidualize a product. Despite all these differences, it can be concluded on the basis of this limited study that it looks like product phases also apply to working-class housing. As is the case with most products, the find-ings reveal that it is difficult to draw a fine line between the end of one product phase and the beginning of the next, and that some product phases overlap one another for long periods of time.

## 4.5 Travelling

Much less written information can be found on the travel sector compared with, for instance, the mobile phone or the bicycle. The information in this section about travelling, and more specifically holiday travel, was therefore largely based on interviews with Ferdinand Fransen and Rob Admiraal[6], on documentation that they made available and on the personal archive of the author of this book[7]. There is a major difference between selling vacations and organizing them. Tour operators or travel organizers assemble and organize the vacation. Travel agencies, operating as agent or as go-between, sell these vacations to the consumer. The introduction of direct selling, mainly via the internet, has changed this process. Because the different activities are not always strictly separate, attention is paid in this section to both activities.

In 1934 Frits Arke and Jan ten Barge started 'Reisbureau Twente'. They borrowed money from their family and had a bus body built on an Opel chassis. The tasks were separated. One day one partner would drive the bus and the other partner would take care of maintenance, and the next day they would change places. They were able to buy a second bus just one year later. Business went well, and both the number of buses and the number of destinations grew. Although they started with trips lasting one day, they were soon offering longer trips to, for instance, Germany, Belgium and France. Fransen's view on the number of competitors was that 'There were a lot of companies that had buses and offered trips. Almost every city had a few companies'.

World War II brought a temporary halt to the growth. At the beginning of the war Reisbureau Twente owned 19 buses. Out of fear for confiscation, 12 of them were dismantled and hidden. In 1943 the Germans ordered that all vehicles that could still be used would become 'sichergestelt' (seized). Another three buses were immediately dismantled, meaning that only four buses were still operational at the end of the war. However, they were not used to any great extent. As Fransen explained, 'Most money was earned by selling coal that was used to power the buses'. Gasoline is no longer available, so the remaining buses were powered by coal gasifiers.

The first few years after the war were quiet in the travel sector. The borders were still closed. However, after a few years, things started to develop very quickly. In the beginning the destinations were still close to the Netherlands, with the popular ones being Belgium, Germany, Austria, France, Italy and Switzerland. Short trips to the Belgian Ardennes and along the river Rhine were also offered.

---

6  F.G. Fransen and R. Admiraal were interviewed on the 14 February 2006. Fransen started his caree in 1944 in 'Reis- en Passagebureau Arke', of which he became owner in 1975 (the name was then 'Arke Reizen'). Admiraal became manager public relations of Arke Reizen in 1973. In 1994 Arke Reizen was sold to the German travel agency TUI.

7  Between 1959 and 1970 the father of Arthur Eger ran a travel agency. Part of the archive of this agency is in his possession.

FIGURE 4.5.1
The first travel guide of OAD.

FIGURE 4.5.2
The travel guide of A. Eger & Zoon from 1959, a stencil duplicated brochure suffices.

FIGURE 4.5.3
Arke travel guide of 1972.

FIGURE 4.5.4
The 'winter sun' and 'far away destinations' guide for the season 1981-1982.

FIGURE 4.5.5
Facade of the 'China shop King Ape' in Amsterdam in 1993. Then a small travel agency specializing in China, Vietnam and Cambodia, nowadays an agency with many 'far away' destinations.

FIGURE 4.5.6
Holidays that don't cost the Earth.

After a conflict between the initiators Arke and Ten Barge, a new agency was started, namely 'Travel and Passage agency Arke' ('Reis- en Passagebureau Arke'). Competitor OAD, founded in 1942 as a consequence of a merger between three small bus companies, introduced its first travel guide in 1952 (Figure 4.5.1). In this brochure 6 afternoon excursions in the direct vicinity (the Province of Overijssel), 24 day trips, 10 two-day trips, 5 three-day trips and 6 longer trips, varying from 8 to 10 days, were offered (De Haan and Van der Vliet, 2005).

In the optimization phase there still was, as was the case in the performance phase, enormous growth in the number of travel agencies. There were specialized agencies that offered scheduled service airline tickets, ship passages, and train tickets, and there were bus companies offering day and holiday trips. However, tobacco shops were also selling holiday trips. The trips were not aimed at a target group, and it seemed that any trip could be sold. A small classified ad in a journal and a stencilled brochure were often enough to entice new clients (Figure 4.5.2). Travellers were inexperienced, and they did not know what to expect, so it was not hard to satisfy their needs. Comparing prices was very difficult because the propositions were very different. However, over time the agencies' documentation was improved. Information was provided about the hotel, apartments or campsites, about the area and the facilities. The facilities themselves were also improved.

Arke designed its first brochure in 1950. Besides trips by bus, train trips and car trips were also offered. The latter market was targeted by A. Eger & Zoon as well from 1958. The destinations were farther away every year. The first trips by boat to Morocco were offered. In the early 1960s, when competition started to grow and more and more people went on holiday in their own car, Fransen (who was 1/3 owner of Arke by then) succeeded in convincing his partners to start becoming involved in air travel. The first air travel to Mallorca was organized in 1965. As Fransen explained:

It took a six hour flight to Mallorca, one of the destinations where sun was guaranteed. For the time being, that was the furthest destination because, travelling any further would involve an expensive stopover having to be made.

Although the first flight was only loss-making for Arke, from 1968 onwards, destinations such as Costa Blanca and later Costa del Sol (Figure 4.5.3) became very profitable. Soon after that, Arke introduced separate guides for car, train, bus, air and youth vacations (Figure 4.5.4).

In the 1958 A. Eger & Zoon travel guide, prices varied between 80 and 200 guilders per week ($40-$100) for between four and eight people. Off-season prices were 25% lower. Over 10 years later, in 1970, the prices had risen to between 150 and 450 guilders ($75-$225). Off-season prices varied between 75 and 150 guilders. This may give the impression that the prices had gone up; however, after correction for inflation, this is not the case. Having said that, the off-season prices were indeed lower.

Going on holiday was no longer an exclusive activity, and most people could afford to take a trip abroad. In addition to the usual car, train, bus and airline vacations, the big tour operators also offered vacations for young people, elderly people and to cities. Often they had specialized guides for different destinations, such as Spain, Portugal and Greece, or for special occasions as winter sports. The most important developments of the 1990s are the intercontinental vacations.

Besides the big tour operators, a niche market has started with small tour operators that cater to a target group or (often exotic) destination (Figure 4.5.5). They organize special vacations for their target groups: adventure travels, cultural travels, city travels, etc. In the segmentation phase the corporate identity gets more and more important: the interior of the office, the quality of the brochures or even the building where the agency is situated need to have an atmosphere that is appreciated by the target group.

For a travel agency the individualization phase is easy to realize. The consumer can decide for himself where he wants to go, for how long, in what kind of accommodation, and which sights he wants to visit. Many of the agencies, which were initially small, specialized in this niche market and often organized individual travels. An internet search on 29 February 2012 for 'individual tours' produced 218,000,000 results. These results include many small, specialized agencies, as well as many big tour operators. In 2006, according to Admiraal, there were about 1,200 big and small travel agencies in a small country like the Netherlands.

In the world of tour operators the awareness phase became relevant over 30 years ago. Consumers became more and more critical with regard to supply. Criticism concerned damage to nature because of ski pistes, damage to Egyptian graves because of the moisture that the enormous number of visitors brings in, and the risk that some kinds of turtles would die out because the beaches they used to lay their eggs were filled with sunbathing tourists. The book *Holidays That Don't Cost the Earth*, which was published in 1992, gives a clear description of this kind of problems (and tries to offer solutions) (Elkington and Hailes, 1992) (Figure 4.5.6).

In this same period the familiar notices appeared in hotels asking you to help protect the environment by throwing used towels onto the floor (or into the bathtub) if you want them changed for clean ones, or by leaving them on the rack if you want to use them again.

## Summary
The history of the travel agency sector also largely followed the theory of product phases. The product characteristic of production was not considered. The documentation was studied for information on the characteristic of styling.

# 5 TECHNOLOGICAL INNOVATION AS AN EVOLUTIONARY PROCESS

*by Huub Ehlhardt*

## 5.1 Introduction

Evolutionary Product Development promotes six product phases that can be used as a guide in the development process of new products. The phases are stages in the development of a product family that have been observed while analyzing how products such as mobile phones, electric shavers and bicycles developed over time. When using the Evolutionary Product Development method it is essential to understand how a product or artefact developed over time.

In biology, the evolutionary history of a species is mapped in a family tree. Different types of family trees are used for different perspectives. Paleontology is the study of prehistoric life, and it uses diagrams called palaeontological trees to map relations between extinct species using fossils as the main source of information. A new type of view on evolutionary relations in biology is based on measuring the genetic distance between species. The longer ago species separated, the greater the genetic distance. This information allows the construction of a so-called phylogenetic tree that maps the genetic relation between species. The phylogenetic tree shows that the Homo sapiens (Humans), the Pan troglodytes (Chimpanzees) and the Gorilla gorilla (Western gorilla) are all closely related. However, humans and chimpanzees are more closely related to each other than to the gorilla. Extinct life forms like the subspecies Homo sapiens neanderthalensis (Neanderthal) form dead-end branches. Current living species are at the foremost tips of branches that are still developing.

Family trees are also used for non-biological phenomena to show evolutionary relations. Linguistics, the scientific study of human languages, uses the language tree to visualize how language families descend from a common ancestor. For example, language trees show that Dutch and Afrikaans are more closely related than Dutch and Frisian, although all belong to the West Germanic language family.

Several authors have discussed evolutionary analogies to product development or innovation. Basalla (1988) described the evolution of hammers, cotton gins, nuclear power reactors and many more. Carlson (2000) documented the invention of an early type of phone by mapping sketches from patent archives and then using them as fossils in a palaeontological tree. Ehlhardt (1995) noted how consumer guides provide a view on the emergence and dissemination of new features in consumer products.

This chapter discusses how one can map the historical development of an artefact in a family tree and thereby depict the evolutionary relations. In order to achieve a better understanding of the development, the situational context or ecosystem is also included. Often a picture can be sketched of influences on the product being developed from the future ecosystem, e.g. by analyzing demographic shifts (such as population aging) or legislation changes (such as the banning of incandescent lamps). Understanding how products came about, what influenced their development, and the elements that will influence their development in the near future is instrumental to Evolutionary Product Development. However, evolution in biology is a blind process. It has no direction because variation is created by random mutation, selection and heredity. One can debate how successful the average product development engineer is in developing products that survive the test of time. In general, one will be tempted to say that the process of product development is not random, but intended to be directed and purposeful. We do not intend to be blind watchmakers,[8] and we therefore want to understand what makes a future product successful and use it to direct the development of new products.

The use of a family tree is a logical method for capturing the historical development of artefacts. The mapping of the ecosystem will facilitate an understanding of historical and likely future influences on the development of the artefact. Mapping a family tree and ecosystem is a valuable addition to the Evolutionary Product Development method described in this book. It will help to establish which product phase is currently applicable to the subject of research.

This chapter provides an example of how a product family of Child Restraint Systems (hereinafter referred to as CRS or CRSs) evolved. In addition, the relationship between the evolving artefact and the ecosystem that co-evolved with it will be explored. The evolutionary relations will be mapped in a product family tree. An explanation will also be given as to how such a product family tree is best constructed as an analytical instrument in Evolutionary Product Development.

8   The term Blind Watchmaker is used to explain that the theory of evolution by natural selection is the only feasible theory capable of explaining the origin of complexity (life) without the intervention of a 'creator' (Dawkins, 1986).

## 5.2  Case Study: Development of Child Restraint Systems

### 5.2.1   Incubation Period

A fundamental reason for the development of CRSs was the presence of cars. The first cars with an internal combustion engine appeared in 1807 and still looked like horse carriages, but with an engine and no horse. These predecessors of today's cars were highly exclusive products. The average young family could not afford them. There was little traffic, the average speed was low and in-car safety was not a major concern. Consequently there was no need for safe CRSs.

The first known example of a product used for restraining small children in cars dates back to 1898 (Smith, 2008). This device did not look like the products that we know today. It was a restraint that was not intended to prevent injuries during accidents, but to keep the children from falling or getting up from their seats when the car was moving.

It took 100 years before large-scale production of cars started. Henry Ford began mass producing cars and the T-Ford came onto the market in 1908. Cars became more affordable, and the number of cars on the road therefore increased, along with the problems we associate with cars today, such as congestion and accidents.

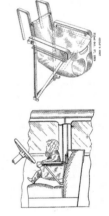

During the interbellum, cars became more common and sources refer to the production of CRSs. Patent files show that various inventors came up with ideas for CRSs. In 1928 a child seat was invented by B. Coleman Silver (Figure 5.2.1) that looked similar to the free hanging CRSs that were common in the second half of the 1960s and early 1970s. These products were intended to keep the child from moving around. Child safety was not the main concern. In the 1930s car safety belts became more prevalent. Slowly but surely, safety in cars started to become an issue, but not as yet for child passengers.

FIGURE 5.2.1
Child's seat invented by
B. Coleman Silver in 1928.

### 5.2.2   Car Safety Features that Have Influenced Child Passenger Safety Expectations

The first safety belt patents date back to the nineteenth century. It was the Swedish inventor, Nils Bohlin who, in 1959, came up with the modern three-point seat belt that is now a standard safety device in most cars. His lap-and-shoulder belt was introduced by Volvo in 1959 and became standard safety equipment for adults in the 1960s. Crash tests proved that these belts saved lives. However, they were met with resistance. Passive safety features such as three-point belts, self-applying belts, front and side-impact air bags, plus active safety such as Anti-lock Braking System (ABS) and Electronic Stability Control (ECS) increased the level of protection for adults. These types of safety equipment became available from 1966 to 1995. The crash safety performance of new cars was tested by the European New Car Assessment Programme (Euro NCAP) and made transparent to consumers. Together, these measures increased the safety consciousness and expectations of consumers and paved the way for safety expectations for CRSs.

### 5.2.3   The First Safety-Focused Child Restraint Seats

The first CRSs which were truly focused on safety were developed in the early 1960s. In 1962 an English couple named Jean Helen and Frederick John Ames invented a padded seat that was strapped against the rear passenger seat (Figure 5.2.2). The child was restrained by a five-point-belt harness that slipped over its head and shoulders and fastened between the legs. The CRS itself was anchored to the car seat with belts. According to the description in the patent, the object of the invention was 'to provide a child's safety seat for vehicles which affords protection for the child comparable to that provided for adults by safety belts and harnesses' (J.H. Ames and F.J. Ames, 1964). The first safety-focused CRS was not a legislation driven product. At that time, relevant legislation was simply not available. The inventors saw an opportunity to improve the safety of children in cars, which was not provided by the belts designed for adults or the CRSs available thus far.

In the 1960s, Swedish car manufacturers, which have a reputation for high safety standards, began to provide CRSs for use in cars. They developed the first rearwards facing type CRS.

### 5.2.4   Initially not All CRSs Were Safe

In 1963, the German manufacturer Storchenmühle launched their first CRS 'Niki' (Figure 5.2.3) onto the market. The product architecture resembles that of Coleman Silver's CRS. The CRS was attached to the car seat by means of a hook. Obviously, this CRS would not remain in place in the event of a collision, and consequently the child passenger would be seriously hurt in the event of a crash. This CRS type was tested and found to be very unsafe during collisions in the 1970 issues of the Dutch consumer guide (Consumentengids, 1970). For that reason the 1974 issue did not include this type in the test (Consumentengids, 1974). Nevertheless, it was still available on the market at the time.

A second model marketed by Storchenmühle was a child restraint that was clamped between the backrest and the (rear passenger) seat (Figure 5.2.4). Similarly to the other Storchenmühle child seat, the child was not safely attached to the seat, nor was the seat rigidly attached to the car. Obviously it would not remain in place during a serious collision. Consumentengids featured this seat in tests in 1970 and again in 1974, when it was described as not providing sufficient protection. Finally the guide advised against the use of this CRS type, describing it as unsafe due to the lack of anchoring to the car in the 1977 issue (Consumentengids, 1977).

Consumer associations recognized early in the 1970s that, to be safe, a CRS needs to be anchored to the car. Such anchoring ensures that the child remains in position during a collision and, further, it benefits

FIGURE 5.2.3
Storchenmühle CRS type
'Niki' introduced in 1963.

FIGURE 5.2.4
The Storchenmühle CRS 'Jet SM 12' 1967,
clamped between the backrest and seat.

FIGURE 5.2.5
Rimo belted harness with
inflatable support.

FIGURE 5.2.7
The Dyn-O-Mite was
imported into Europe
and sold as the first
Maxi-Cosi.

FIGURE 5.2.9
The safe fit belt adapter designated
unsafe by Consumentenbond.

FIGURE 5.2.10
The Maxi-Cosi Pebble above a
Maxi-Cosi FamilyFix base with
light and sound controls for
correct installation and semi-
universal Isofix.

from the energy absorption system of the car. An interesting concept with anchoring was the CRS type of the Rimo brand (Figure 5.2.5). It consists of a belt harness connected to the car supported by an inflatable seat. In the 1970 issue of *Consumentengids*, this is the only CRS type for children up to 2 years (out of 17 tested …) for which the test report mentioned that, if a child was belted into its seat, no injury would be expected during a collision (Consumentengids, 1970). Curiously, the product disappeared from the test, and probably also from the market a few years later.

The 1970 test of CRSs in *Consumentengids* describes 17 different CRS types for children up to two years and 5 CRS types for children between two and six years by a total of 17 brands. In 1977 this increased to 18 brands and 29 different types. The number of CRSs available on the Dutch market increased.

## 5.2.5   Consumer Guides Start Influencing Legislation

The increasing use of cars, the related increase in accidents and the presence of CRSs that actually provided some safety created a climate in which legislation started to develop from the early 1970s onwards. In the USA, articles in consumer guides also influenced CRS development. A 1972 issue of Consumer Reports, the American consumer guide published by the Consumers Union, mentions that most car CRSs that passed the FMVSS 213 legislation (which was the Federal Standard for CRS enforced in the USA at that time) could not withstand crash tests. In 1975 this led to a proposal for revising the regulation issued in 1971. With the USA having a history as a single constitutional entity dating back to the end of the eighteenth century and Europe still struggling to form one, it will come as no surprise to read that child safety legislation was also harmonized in the USA earlier than in Europe. It would take until 1981 for ECE-44-01, the first European CRS legislation, to be introduced. Since then legislation from both the European Union (EU) and the USA has played a major role in requirements imposed on the design and use of CRSs.

The development of CRS legislation and CRS products is closely intertwined. CRS legislation did not result in the invention of the first safety-focused CRS, but was developed after the products had appeared on the market. However, the continuous development of CRS legislation in both the USA and the EU set the legal scene for increasing requirements imposed on CRSs. Along with the development of CRSs as a product family, an increasing body of knowledge on (mis)usage developed. Child-passenger safety advocacy groups, consumer associations and standardization programmes have encouraged governments to continue renewing safety legislation. The resulting current level sets a threshold for minimal safety functionality for CRSs well above what was achieved by the best performing CRS in the early 1970s. CRS legislation co-evolved with the CRS products.

### 5.2.6   Legislation Starts to Influence CRS Design

The legislative changes in the USA in 1975 led to heavy, and therefore difficult to handle, CRSs and this prompted designer Paul K. Meeker to develop an easier to handle CRS (Figure 5.2.6). The resulting CRS was sold by Questor Corporation as the Infanseat 440 or the Dyn-O-Mite. The reclining seat could be used for different activities like sleeping, feeding, playing and as a car seat. It was a rearwards facing CRS using the belt to secure it to the car seat.

FIGURE 5.2.6
Baby carrier and car seat, patent 4,231,612 filed in September 1978 by Paul K. Meeker.

In 1977 Sjef van der Linden, a Dutch entrepreneur in baby articles, saw the Dyn-O-Mite in Macy's store in Manhattan while on a business trip to the USA (Dorel, 2005). Recognizing the potential of this product to fill the void in the European market he started discussing the possibility of importing the seat with Questor Corporation.

A couple of years later, he started selling the product in Europe. The first version was supplied by an Italian concession holder, Babymex Italiana. However, this product failed in crash tests at the Dutch contract research institute TNO. It appeared to use a different and more brittle type of plastic, which was sufficient in Italy, where it was not used as a car seat. The plastic type was changed and the design improved with the help of a Swedish test institute and a Dutch designer. From 1985 onwards, the product was sold in Europe under the name Maxi-Cosi (Figure 5.2.7). This signaled the start of the currently dominant baby CRS in the Netherlands.

The Dutch consumer guide observed in a 1983 issue that there was still no proper CRS for the smallest children (Consumentengids, 1983). The carrycot used for babies was described as a product that did not properly fulfill its safety function. In the event of collisions the belt might cut through the thin sides of the carrycot. Besides this, any child that is not belted inside the carrycot would be slung so hard through the device that he or she would sustain injuries. In 1987 Consumentenbond (Consumentengids, 1987) published a first review that included the Maxi-Cosi and mentioned that CRSs were finally starting to become available that would really qualify as safety seats for babies. This took a quarter century from the invention of the first safety-focused CRS (...).

### 5.2.7   Types Come and Go

In the 1980s *Consumentengids* continued to question the functionality of various CRSs types. One issue (Consumentengids, 1983) described the belt harness as an outdated restraint type. In the event of collisions, children of six years and older would slide into the lap part of the harness and might slip under it ('submarine'). This could cause severe damage to the liver, kidneys and spleen of the child passenger. The arrival of a new, safer CRS type for children, the booster cushion, was welcomed as an improvement in child safety. This booster cushion is a seat type without a backrest that elevates the child in such a way that it can use the three-point belt. It is aimed at children in the age group 3 to 10.

The belt harness with its apparent low position in the competitive landscape disappeared from subsequent reviews in the *Consumentengids*. Reports like these helped increase consumer awareness of what makes a good CRS and what not, and therefore also influenced sales.

### 5.2.8 Perception of CRS Change and Categorization Starts/Dominant Design Directions Emerge

Literature such as consumer guides reflect changes through time of the perception of CRSs and how they should be used. Changing categorization is one example of this.

In the 1970s, *Consumentengids* only distinguished between Child Seats and Child Belts. The seats were for children up to 3 years old. Children aged between 3 and 6 were supposed to wear belt-type restraints. In the 1980s, the *Consumentengids* tests started to provide an overview of the different products, categorized into age groups. Following changes in legislation, the 1983 article on CRSs distinguished between the following age and product groups: up to 9 months (cradles), about 9 months to 5 years (seats), about 3 to 10 years (booster cushions) and finally about 4 to 12 years the harness belts. The 1984 article on CRSs adds weight classes to these age groups (Consumentengids, 1984).

The article on CRSs published in the 1990 issue of *Consumentengids* mentions, for the first time, an age group system that is aligned with the ECE legislation (Consumentengids, 1990). It uses four groups (0/0+, 1, 2, 3) with progressive weight groups and corresponding age classes (see also Figure 5.2.8). This weight and age classification system has been used up to today.

The same review states that the manufacturers of CRSs were trying to develop seats that can be used for longer and cover various continuous age groups. Unfortunately they were not very successful. Within a few years the situation improved. Three years later, the guide (Consumentengids, 1993) was more positive and stated that several manufacturers sold CRSs covering age groups 2 to 3 that functioned fairly well, although those targeted at covering age groups 1 to 3 still performed rather poorly.

FIGURE 5.2.8
Overlapping age & weight groups.

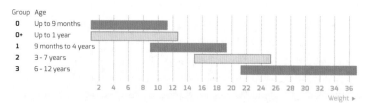

### 5.2.9 Coincidence Influences CRS Legislation

In 1994 the three-year-old Dana Hutchinson from the USA was killed after being struck by an airbag deployed while in a rearwards facing CRS in the passenger seat (Colella, 2010). During the investigation into why the CRS had not prevented fatal injuries her relatives found out that the vehicle seating position and the CRS that was secured in it were incompatible. The case received huge attention in the USA, and resulted in the formation of a child passenger safety advocacy group called the Drivers Appeal for National Awareness (DANA) Foundation by Joseph Colella (an uncle of Dana) and relatives. The goal of this non-profit organization is to raise public awareness of incompatibilities and misuse, and to collaborate with manufacturers and regulators on simplifying the correct use of child restraints. DANA successfully advocated legislation changes, which made warning labels on CRSs and airbag cut-off switches for cars obligatory.

## 5.2.10 Focus Shifts to Details

In general, CRSs still provide less protection than was possible and desired in the early 1990s. One of the reasons is that they do not go well with modern cars and standard seat belts. Cars sold from 1990 onwards need to have safety belts available for the back seats. Once three-point belts had become common for rear seats, CRSs needed to adapt to this situation. Unfortunately, Dutch legislation of the early 1990s still allowed for 'unsafe transportation' of children. The use of a CRS was only obligatory if available. Children aged three to twelve could use belts if present whether those were lap belts or three-point belts. And if no belts were available at all, they were still allowed to travel at the back seat (Consumentengids, 1993).

In 1993 the Safe Fit belt adapter was sold as a CRS, which competed with booster seats (Figure 5.2.9). According to Consumentenbond (Consumentengids, 1993), this belt adapter should never have received the ECE-44 approval as it is unsafe. Consumentenbond requested clarification from the Minister of Traffic and Road Safety with regard to the assessment of approval for this particular belt adapter, and it subsequently disappeared from the market.

Once the dominant designs for CRSs started appearing in the 1980s and car safety features improved, the focus of articles in Consumentengids shifted in the 1990s from descriptions of new and improved CRS types to an emphasis on comfort and proper use. The focus was on a comfortable and convenient CRS both for children to sit in and for the parents who have to install them. As surveys show that more than half the CRSs are not installed correctly, the Dutch consumer guide underlines the need for proper manuals (Consumentengids, 1993). Apparently, the designs are still not sufficiently self-explanatory, and written instructions are still required.

Additional CRS safety and comfort features were introduced after 2000. One example is Isofix, which makes it easier to install the CRS (see also the section on standardization). Maxi-Cosi started to market a product called the FamilyFix, which is connected to the car via Isofix connectors (Figure 5.2.10). Parents can simply snap in a Maxi-Cosi on top of the FamilyFix. The product uses electronics to indicate with a visual and auditory signal whether the CRS is connected correctly to the base. This ensures properly installed seats and therefore increases safety.

More and more manufacturers started adding so-called 'side wings' to CRSs that helped protect the child more effectively against injuries caused by the impact of a side collision. Legislation did not (yet) require these provisions, but consumer guides did assign a better score to products that had these side wings. Helleke Hendriks, one of the researchers at Consumentenbond, claims that this was down to their reviews; 'Our demanding tests are thus market guiding, as legislation does not require these side wings' (Consumentengids, 2010).

Several brands stopped producing booster cushions without backrests, as these do not protect children sufficiently from injuries caused by side impacts. The extent to which this change of course can be attributed to the success of the consumer association(s) remains unclear.

## 5.2.11 Standardization and Safety Programme Organizations

Euro NCAP has carried out child occupant safety assessments since its inception to ensure that manufacturers take responsibility for children travelling in vehicles produced by them. In November 2003, Euro NCAP introduced a child occupant protection rating to make it easier for consumers to understand the outcome of these tests. In these assessments, Euro NCAP used dummies sized as 18 months and 3-year-old children in the frontal- and side-impact tests. Apart from studying the results of the impact tests, Euro NCAP assessed the clarity of instructions for seat installation in the vehicle.

In 1990 the International Organization for Standardization (ISO) launched the Isofix standard in an attempt to provide a standard for fixing car seats into different makes of car. The system consists of a male connector on the CRS and a female connector in the car seat. The US equivalent of this system is called Lower Anchors and Tethers for Children (LATCH).

Obviously, to be of any use, this system needs to be adapted by manufacturers of cars and those of CRSs. Consequently, the proliferation of this feature in CRSs (the fitness in evolutionary language) is dependent on the extent to which car manufacturers implement these connectors throughout their fleet. It took about a decade of discussions with the automotive industry before all involved agreed to the technical specifications. The current version of the standard was published in 1999. Some CRS manufacturers had started selling Isofix-compliant baby car seats in the EU from around 2000. The EU regulations required cars from 2009 to be fitted with Isofix anchorage points. As cars in EU countries until the 2004 expansion were, on average, 8.5 years old (ACEA, 2009) this meant, with the average age remaining constant, that it would take slightly less than a decade, or until 2018, before half the cars on the road were compulsorily equipped with Isofix. This sets the scene for the market adoption rate of Isofix in CRSs sold to consumers in the EU.

The phasing in of LATCH in the USA was completed in 2002. Assuming that the average age and life expectancy of cars in the USA are similar to those in the EU, this means that 8.5 years later (at the beginning of 2011) LATCH would be compulsorily installed in the majority of cars on US roads. It could therefore be expected that LATCH would become the default installation method about seven years before Isofix reaches the same level as in the EU.

The European Association for the Co-ordination of Consumer Representation in Standardization (ANEC), a European organization involved in standardization of consumer products, influenced legislation and standardization of CRS. Since 2006, the organization (ANEC, 2006) has advocated an increase in the age up to which children are seated backwards from the current 9 to 15 months or 16.5 kg, as this increases the safety during frontal collision.

Furthermore, the ANEC promotes a stature-based system referred to as I-size to replace the current weight-based system (ANEC, 2011). CRS in this system refers to the minimal and maximum child length for the seat to fit. Further I-size requires rearward-facing transport until the child is 15 months of age and provide side impact protection. The I-size regulation will be implemented from 2013 and eventually all old style CRS will disappear from the market (ANEC, 2012).

## 5.2.12  Consumer Associations

Consumer associations played a pivotal role in the advancement of CRSs. In many countries, consumer associations have been founded in line with the advancement of the consumer society. Comparative tests are a key feature of their magazines, the so-called consumer guides. Consumer guides frequently report on CRSs. For example, *Consumentengids* featured an initial article on CRSs in 1970. Until 2010 the magazine published a total of 18 comparative tests. In these articles the performance of different CRSs available on the market at the time of writing were compared and discussed. Particularly in the 1970s and early 1980s, these products did not often perform well as regards their primary functionality, namely to ensure safety during collisions for children travelling in cars.

Consumer guides provide an independent and detailed overview of the quality and price of the products available in the market in the comparative tests. Pictures of articles tested, and relevant references to legislation, importers, and manufacturers are included. This makes them an excellent source of information for analyzing the historical development of consumer goods. Products that perform best are designated 'best choice'. Producers often use these qualifications in their marketing, and retailers display copies of such articles at point of sale. Consumer associations therefore directly influence the purchasing behaviour of consumers and, in that way, exert evolutionary pressure (selection of the fittest).

Consumer associations also directly address legislators and manufacturers as described in an article by Consumentenbond, which mentions the use of video recordings of crash tests with CRSs. These videos have been shown to both legislators and manufacturers in order to convince them that there was a need to improve the standards with which the CRSs should comply (Consumentengids, 1993). An example of the arguments used was that CRSs should not be tested with a lap belt, but with the retractable three-point belt instead. Those new requirements have subsequently been described in the ECE-44-03 legislation.

Consumer associations of various countries are united in different bodies such as ANEC, Consumers International (a federation of consumer groups) and International Consumer Research and Testing (ICRT) that focus on joint research and comparative testing. Consumer associations cooperate on product tests and share information used to compile the reviews published. Employees of various consumer associations participate in bodies like ANEC for which they publish research into CRSs' safety with the objective to influence legislation and standardization (ANEC, 2003). Along these routes the different international consumer associations cooperate and influence both legislation such as ECE-44 and standardization issues such as Isofix and I-size. Consumentenbond claims that this cooperation between various consumer associations in Europe has led to increasingly safe CRSs (Consumentengids, 1994).

### 5.2.13  Increasing Scale at Manufacturers Reduces Regional Design Differences

Similarly to cars and other consumer goods, regional differences can be found in people's preference for a specific technology, product architecture or design language. In the USA the larger car models like SUVs and trucks are widely sold. In Europe, where fuel has traditionally been taxed more heavily, the average car is smaller and more fuel efficient than in the USA. Similar differences can be observed for CRS. In Scandinavia, rearwards facing CRS are promoted for up to four years. Other parts in Europe will adapt to a new length-based standard (I-size) that increases current rearwards facing from 9 to 15 months or 16.5 kg.

Over the decades a large number of companies have been involved in the development and production of CRSs. Historically they served different geographical markets. In recent years mergers and acquisitions caused a consolidation on the CRS market. Currently, only a few large players remain. In Europe several large companies, plus a few smaller ones, and white label products from Asia now serve the market. Dorel is a Canadian firm that acquired Maxi-Cosi, which primarily sells in Central and Western Europe, and Bebé-Comfort which is traditionally strong around the Mediterranean. Britax Römer is an Anglo-German firm that, besides its own brand, also supplies CRSs to various automotive manufacturers that sell them under their own brand. Storchenmühle was originally a German manufacturer and is now owned by the globally operating Keiper Recaro Group that specializes in mobile seating. HTS (Hans Torgersen & Sønn AS), traditionally strong in Scandinavia, targets the European and Asian markets. These larger CRS manufacturers all have their own in-house development centres where they consolidate resources and know-how to develop new products.

The scale increase in the CRS market, the international trade with ever more global companies, and the Information Age mean that knowledge of CRS disseminates more quickly now than it did in the early 1970s. Although design differences remain, these differences will gradually become smaller.

## 5.3 Perspectives on the Development of CRSS

### 5.3.1 Using Tree Diagrams

In linguistics, that is, the scientific study of human languages, family tree diagrams have been used for decades to show the historical relations between languages in a single picture (Southworth, 1964). For the historical development of artefacts a tree diagram is not as common. As W. Bernard Carlson (2000) showed in his article on the development of the telephone by Edison, the process of invention and development of artefacts can also be mapped as a tree diagram. In the case studied in his article, the development of a new and better type of telephone by Edison, the point of departure was a phone model developed by Alexander Graham Bell. Edison did not work on the development of the improved telephone on his own. Along with several assistants he worked as part of a team on models, sketches, etc. The sketches produced by this team were ranked by Carlson (and team) into a palaeontological tree that visualizes the consecutive stages of development of the telephone.

### 5.3.2 Mapping the Development of CRSS in a Product Family Tree

A similar tree-like diagram can also be used to map the development of the CRSS (Figure 5.3.1). As shown above, the CRSS did not originate at once, but evolved over a century from numerous seats from the hands of a 'collective body of inventors', a varied group of people such as designers, salesmen and test laboratory employees. As similarly remarked by Badke-Schaub (2007) on the subject of scientific discovery, CRS have been shown to develop in incremental steps, based on past experience.

It is important to note the influence of external events, such as the development of cars, safety belts, legislation and the death of Dana Hutchinson, on the development of CRSS. These factors constitute the ecosystem and were crucial for the development of CRSS over time.

Figure 5.3.1 shows the development of CRSS into different dominant designs. Because the purpose of the diagram is to explain the evolution of CRSS into a family of products, it is referred to as the Product Family Tree (PFT). The second half of the 1960s and the early 1970s was a period of rapidly increasing complexity and diversity in these child seats. Like a Cambrian explosion, the diversity of CRSS rapidly increased. Several

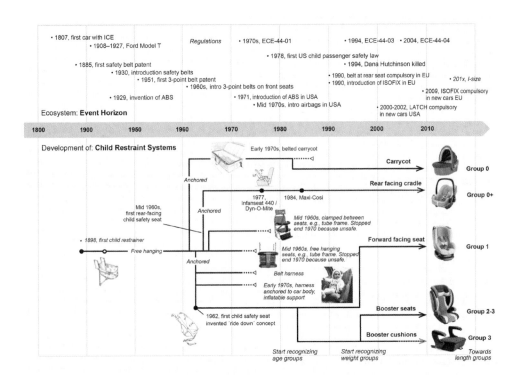

FIGURE 5.3.1
The product family tree of CRSS. (For an enlarged image, see page 140)

designs proved to be unsafe and, although they subsequently became extinct, they still influenced legislation. Other designs provided better protection and evolved into the dominant designs we know today.

The evolution of CRSS led to three different dominant designs catering to different market segments (based on age, weight or length). The first is the cradle type, in which babies and toddlers aged up to 1.5 years or weighing up to 12 kg lie rearwards facing in a reclined position. The second is the seat type for small children aged up to seven or weighing up to 24 kg. Both these types have their own belt harnesses for children whose bone structure, muscles and length are not yet mature enough to use the three-point-belt for adults provided in the car. The third, the booster type for children aged up to 12 years or weighing up to 36 kg, does not have a belt system of its own and uses the three-point-belt provided in the car. The evolution of the product reached the segmentation phase as described in Chapter 3 of this book.

### 5.3.3 Relation between Development of Artifact and Ecosystem

As noted in this chapter, the interaction between the development of artefact and ecosystem shaped the development of both. Other authors noticed similar systems and discussed the development of artefacts in niches, which are influenced by developments in the wider ecosystem or socio-technical regimes and industrial landscapes (Joore, 2010). The role of legislation as an important element of these socio-technical regimes

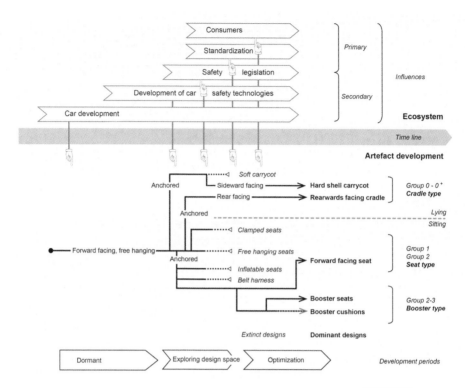

FIGURE 5.3.2
The relation between
artefact and ecosystem.
(For an enlarged image,
see page 141)

is discussed in connection with the development of forms of sustainable transport (Hoogema et al., 2002; Van den Hoed, 2004).

Figure 5.3.2 depicts this mutual relation. The lower half shows the developmental relations between different CRS types. The upper half summarizes the ecosystem that interacted with the CRSs as they developed over time. A strong and mutual influence on the development of CRSs has been observed between CRSs on the one hand and consumers (including consumer associations and advocacy groups), standardization and CRSs-related legislative bodies on the other. This has been described as a primary influence in Figure 5.3.2. An indirect or secondary influence on the development of CRSs has been observed from the wider environment of general car safety legislation, car safety technology development and general car development.

CRSs have come a long way in terms of the safety they provide, their ease of use and their comfort. In general, one can say that the current CRSs perform well as regards their primary function, namely to provide safety to child passengers in cars during driving, in general, and in the event of a collision, in particular.

The designs sold in the Netherlands have conceptually been stable over the last two decades. That does not mean that evolution has halted. The current major review in standardization by the ANEC (towards I-size, a stature-based system promoting rearwards facing until 15 months), the room for improvement in side-impact protection, the relatively high levels of incorrectly installed CRSs and the lack of support for booster-only cushions mean that further evolution can be expected.

International developments in, for example, safety legislation, international trade and the consolidation amongst manufacturers have been important evolutionary forces for CRSs. It can therefore be expected that identical or similar evolutionary forces affected CRSs in different habitats, leading to rather similar dominant designs. In the end, CRSs in other countries have to comply with the same or similar legislation, are used for children of the same age, weight and length classes and are being used in cars sold around the globe.

## 5.4  Product Family Tree for Use in Evolutionary Product Development Context

### 5.4.1  Why Use It

As has been shown in the example for CRSs, mapping the historical development of a product in a PFT, together with the ecosystem that interacted and co-evolved with it, facilitates an understanding of the evolution of the product (Figures 5.3.1 and 5.3.2). Any development in products or other artefacts builds on previous developments. For that reason, understanding how a product came about, what influenced the development in the past, and what will influence its future are instrumental when developing a successful next-generation product.

### 5.4.2  How to Construct One

In order to draw a PFT a thorough understanding of the historical development is required. Sources like patents provide a detailed description of the innovative art of the invention concerned. They also contain a clear time stamp and often references to prior art, which means earlier related inventions. Patents are becoming easily accessible via the Internet, and reviewing them is part of the standard homework for any new product development team. For a lot of products there is legislation via which the development can be traced and – importantly – upcoming changes identified. Depending on the type of product, books, catalogues or consumer guides provide further historical (or more up-to-date) information.

The collected information can be used to construct a PFT diagram. The points where branches split are markers for changes in technology, product architecture and/or dominant designs that have to be identified in the upfront analysis. Unfortunately the level of familiarity cannot be calculated as in polygenetic trees that are constructed on the basis of genetic distance. Constructing a PFT is a trial-and-error process (like any design), in which various types of diagrams can be used (Figure 5.4.1).

While collecting information that is used to construct the tree-like diagram, one will come across information about the ecosystem or

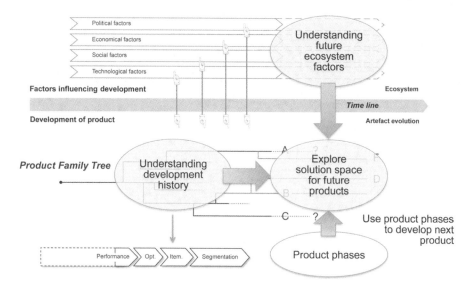

FIGURE 5.4.1
Possible PFT diagrams mapping the product evolution.

environment that influenced the development of the product. There are tools and methods that can be used to make sure different relevant perspectives are included. One of them is PEST, which is an acronym describing the types of perspectives useful for this analysis: Political, Economic, Social and Technological:

- Political covers, for example product safety laws (such as for CRSs) or legislation used to ban the incandescent lamp.
- Economic covers, for example rising oil prices, high prices for copper, falling purchasing power in times of economic crisis or increasing purchasing power in rising economies.
- Social covers, for example demographic shifts such as retiring baby boomers or increasing urbanization.
- Technical, the most obvious perspective in this context, covers inventions such as the transistor and standardization such as USB3.0 or WiFi.

The information of the artefact evolution and ecosystem is combined in one picture separated by a time line. Together with the product phases, they help product developers explore the solution space for future products (Figure 5.4.2).

FIGURE 5.4.2
Using the product family tree to explore the solution space for future products.

# EPRO TOOL.[9]

*by Ferry Vermeulen*

## 6.1 Introduction

Small and medium-sized enterprises (SMEs) are generally considered to be an important vehicle for new product development and innovation. Innovation is generally regarded as necessary for the creation of a sustainable competitive advantage, which itself is an essential element in a company's survival strategy. However, SMEs inherently experience specific problems in their innovation processes, for example by pursuing strategies that build on operational capabilities, which negatively influence their average innovative performance. To increase the chance of success of an innovation generated by an SME, it would be best to choose step-by-step strategies. The theory of product phases can be used to make overall predictions for the evolutionary development of a product after its market introduction and to formulate low-risk strategies. This theory has been transformed into a 'diagnosis tool', which offers fresh starting points for innovation strategies by SMEs. The tool (a computer program) consists of a questionnaire that is used to analyze the present situation of a company and to give possible strategies for future development of the product. The tool has been developed in cooperation with several companies and has been tested by students at the University of Twente.

This chapter briefly describes the background to, and the operation of, the tool. Section 6.2 describes the phenomenon that is often referred to as the 'innovation paradox'. Section 6.3 describes the perspectives of the tool. Section 6.4 describes the development of the tool. Section 6.5 is a summary of instructions on how to use the tool. Section 6.5.4 of this chapter gives an example of the output of the tool.

## 6.2 The Innovation Paradox

In the past few decades there has been an increasing focus on the need for permanent innovation in SMEs. Worldwide, SMEs have been accepted as the engine of economic growth and of the promotion of equitable development. Successful SMEs are recognized as being an important

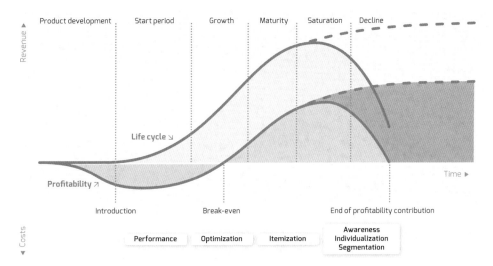

Revenue ▲

Costs ▼

| Product development | Start period | Growth | Maturity | Saturation | Decline |

Life cycle ↘

Profitability ↗

Time ►

Introduction                Break-even                End of profitability contribution

| Performance | Optimization | Itemization | Awareness Individualization Segmentation |

FIGURE 6.2.1
The Product Life Cycle.

component of industrial development, and its consequent social benefits for all economies (Daniel et al., 2008). Since the European Commission formulated their 'Lisbon' strategy in 2000, in which the European Council aimed to develop the European Union to the most dynamic and competitive (knowledge-based) economies in 2010, national governments have paid more and more attention to innovation (De Jong, 2004).

Innovation is generally considered as a necessity for the creation of a sustainable competitive advantage, which itself is an essential element of a company's survival strategy.

The (economic) Product Life Cycle (PLC) plays a central role in this consideration (Figure 6.2.1). After a certain period of time, a product will disappear from the market because a better product that fulfils the same needs has been introduced or because consumer requirements have changed. The product has reached its peak and is descending towards the 'end phase'. Quite often this is the result of product introductions by competitors and a loss of distinctive properties. Price competition will increase, and that will create an even greater need for product renewal. Although market circumstances (the level of competitiveness), the time interval and the speed of turnover growth can vary significantly in the various product phases for different products and given that the duration of the total PLC can vary from a couple of weeks to many decades, after a certain period a downward trend of the PLC will become visible, which is the main reason for the need for permanent innovation (Korbijn, 1999).

Despite the chances innovation can offer companies, SMEs, in particular, have specific problems in their innovation process that negatively influence their overall innovation performance (Pullen et al., 2009). Innovations from SMEs seem to be limited by the 'gap' between the generation of knowledge and the implementation of this knowledge by the businesses, the so-called innovation paradox. The innovation paradox is the inability or reluctance of manufacturing firms (especially SMEs) to pursue strategies that build the operational capabilities necessary for innovation that will lead to both profitability and growth (Deloitte Research, 2004).

Several reasons are given for this innovation paradox. A lack of resources to invest substantially on a permanent basis in R&D is given as the main reason (Risseeuw and Thurik, 2003; Tanje, 2004). Although not all SMEs work intensively on innovation, many examples can be found that show that innovation can be a major force when it comes to developing SMEs into bigger companies (e.g. companies like Microsoft, Google and ASML). Several studies can be found in the literature in which a relation has been found between innovation and a company's performance. Klomp and Van Leeuwen (1999) conclude that the growth in turnover for companies that innovate is bigger than that for their non-innovating colleagues. The same also seems to apply to SMEs. Despite this, it is quite often assumed that innovation will always pay off. Some innovations will turn out to be ineffective and potentially effective innovations will not be realized. If we divide all innovations into revolutionary and evolutionary innovations, history shows us that revolutionary innovations in particular seem to unravel most often. Some historically unravelled innovations are the Apple Lisa (1983), Video 2000 by Philips and Grundig (1979), DCC by Philips (1991), Minidisc by Sony (1992) and the Peugeot 106 Electrique (1995). Although it is easier to gain media attention with revolutionary innovations and the adventure and rewards seem more interesting and promising, evolutionary innovations are a much safer option. Especially for SMEs, non-successful innovations can imply considerable risks for the future development of a company.

## 6.3  An Evolutionary Approach

To increase the chance of success of complex problems – and innovation undoubtedly is a complex phenomenon – it would be best to choose step-by-step strategies (Ansoff, 1965; Popper, 1957; Schumpeter, 1934). The strategies described in the literature have strong evolutionary characteristics. In several disciplines in which studies into innovation processes have been carried out, such as economics and the research into technological development, which is closely related to economics, a deterministic point of view has gradually been replaced during the last few decades by an evolutionary point of view. If we examine the design practice, the experience is that most of the design projects that are carried out concern evolutionary product changes.

The fact that the chance of success is higher for Evolutionary Product Development can be explained by several models. One of these models is the model for growth strategies (Ansoff, 1965). This model (see Figure 6.3.1) shows several growth strategies and their chance of success. To increase the chance of success it is best to choose strategies relating

FIGURE 6.3.1
Grow strategies according to
Ansoff; and their chances of
success.

|                  | Existing products               | New products                        |
|------------------|----------------------------------|-------------------------------------|
| Existing markets | **Market penetration** (-90%)    | **Product development** (-25%)      |
| New markets      | **Market development** (-50%)    | **Diversification** (between 1-7%)  |

to existing products (according to Ansoff, existing products also include products with small product changes). As an indication, the model shows that the chance of success when putting an existing product on an existing or new market is about 50%-90%. Totally new products score much lower (1%-25%).

The model relating to the adoption behaviour of consumers can also be used to indicate that evolutionary innovations can be more successful. The model states that to increase the chance of success, an innovation has to have enough added value for its user, must not be technologically complex and must fit into existing systems. Sometimes there is only a small increase in the added value of an evolutionary innovation. However, evolutionary innovations are almost never technologically complex and fit mostly in existing systems. On the other hand, the added value of revolutionary innovations is quite often distinctly present. Despite this, the chance of success decreases as these innovations are mostly technologically complex and do not fit into existing systems.

This can be best explained by some examples. About a decade ago, electric cars were much more revolutionary than they are nowadays. Today an electric car contributes to both a better world and to your wallet. Ten years ago, the combination of a new technique with little sales meant that the price of an electric car was much higher than it is today. Despite the fact that the fuel an electric car uses is very cheap, their purchase price was way too high for many consumers (e.g. the average price of an electric car around 2000 was about €30,000-€40,000). The only added value for people in those times, or at least in their opinion, would have been a contribution to a better environment, which unfortunately was not enough added value for most of them.

Besides this, because the technology used in electric cars was relatively new – or at least much less developed – cars did not have a wide range in those days. For example the range of the Peugeot 106 Electrique was about 80 km. Another technical shortcoming was its charging time, which exceeded eight hours. Finally, the lack of charging possibilities meant that an electric car did not fit in well with existing systems.

Nowadays electric cars are on sale for less than €9,000. According to Nissan, the Nissan Leaf's expected all-electric range is 160 km. Electric cars can be charged within 30 minutes (in the near future charging times of 10 minutes are expected) and charging points are becoming more and more prevalent (with their number increasing all the time). The chance of success when introducing an electric car on the market is nowadays much bigger.

Despite the opportunities Evolutionary Product Development can offer companies, very little is known about it. Karl Popper's theory about piecemeal engineering does show similarities. In this theory he discusses the improvement of society rationally by step-by-step improvements, rather than a search for Utopias. The Kaizen philosophy also shows similarities to Evolutionary Product Development. Kaizen is Japanese for 'improvement', or 'change for the better' and refers to philosophy or practices that focus on continuous improvement of processes in manufacturing, engineering and business management.

One way to formulate step-by-step innovation strategies is based on the theory of the product phases developed by Eger (2007). According to Eger, product phases can be used to make overall predictions for the evolutionary development of a product after its market introduction (see Chapter 3). The question is whether it is possible to transform the theory of product phases into a tool, and, if so, whether the tool offers fresh starting points for innovation strategies by SMEs. If it is possible to develop a tool, based on the theory of product phases, such a tool will have several different perspectives. First of all, it will be possible to shorten the time to market of a product. Second, it will be possible to describe, in a more qualitative manner, the future development of the product in time. As a result, it will be possible to develop products with added value that the consumer appreciates more than competitive similar products. Third, a tool will help designers and entrepreneurs in their decision-making processes. Fourth, the tool will provide an insight into a complex matter. For example, innovation is characterized by trial and error, which makes an innovation process expensive. The tool means the process could occur in a more structured (and more inexpensive) way.

The expected result of the research will be an innovation tool for SMEs, based on the model of product phases, to help them determine the status quo and future of a company's product. In this way innovation strategies for the future development of a product can be made. Besides the economic Product Life Cycle (see Section 6.2), very little is known about the development of products after market introduction. No tools have been found that describe in a qualitative manner how a product should evolve after its market introduction. Because in design practice most product innovations relate to small product changes/evolutionary improvements, the tool can be a helpful instrument for the designer or entrepreneur

## 6.4  The Development of the Tool

### 6.4.1  Research Questions

Research has been carried out into the possibilities to transform the theory of product phases into a useful tool. The purpose of the first part of the research was to investigate whether it is possible for entrepreneurs and product managers to determine the product phase of their product with the help of the statements as described in Evolutionary Product Development. The purpose of the second part of the research was to investigate whether it is possible to use the collected data to formulate fresh and useful starting points for the future development of a product. To this end the research has been split into two phases: a pilot and an extended research. The main purpose of the pilot was to explore the topic area. To test the feasibility, the observations were described and analyzed to improve the method for the extended research.

In order to investigate whether it is possible for entrepreneurs and product managers to determine the product phase of their product and, secondly, whether the collected data can be used to formulate fresh and useful starting points for the future development of a product, the following research questions will be answered:

1   When statements, as described in Evolutionary Product Development, have been transformed into questions and are put into a questionnaire, is it possible for an entrepreneur to determine the product phase of a product?
2.  Can the collected data be used to formulate fresh and useful starting points for innovation strategies (by adding the product characteristics of the next product phase)?
3.  Is it possible to transform the theory of product phases into a useful tool that offers fresh starting points for innovation strategies?

### 6.4.2   The Pilot

First, the statements as described in Evolutionary Product Development (Eger, 2007) have been transformed into questions and put into a questionnaire. As the first goal of the research was to investigate whether it is possible for entrepreneurs and product managers to determine the product phase of their product, the unit of analysis is the entrepreneur or product manager. The participants are characterized by the fact that they have good knowledge of the companies' own products. They are involved on a day-to-day basis in the development of the product and the strategies to be taken. Research was carried out by means of the questionnaire, and a first pilot with five companies and their entrepreneurs or product managers has been set up. Because the ultimate primary goal is to evolve the product and to strengthen the competitive position of the company, the companies were asked to identify two competitive products and answer the same questions for these products as well. The result is the determination of the product phase of the participating companies and the product phases of two competitive products.

The second goal of the research is to investigate whether it is possible to use the results from the questionnaire to formulate fresh and useful starting points for the future development of a product. Therefore the answers to the questionnaires have been incorporated into a product data sheet. These strategies provide a direction for the company (or product designer) with regard to what should be done with the product on the following 18 aspects:

1   Newness
2   Functionality and reliability
3   Technology
4   Number of parts
5   Ergonomics
6   Safety
7   Assortment/is there much choice?
8   Adaptability to consumer wishes and ethics
9   Product development
10  Styling
11  Integration of form
12  Number of competitors
13  Price
14  Production
15  Assembly
16  Promotion
17  Influence of the consumer on the final product
18  Service organization

The questionnaire appeared to be an adequate method for determining the product phase of a company's product. However, several shortcomings have been found as well that should be avoided in future research. The participating companies have been asked to comment on every starting point and to evaluate it. In general, all the participating companies were positive about the results and willing to follow some of the suggestions. During the time that the results were evaluated, two companies continued innovating their products and used some of the formulated starting points (without knowing the results of the questionnaire).

Because of the perspectives of the research and with the pilot as useful input, the materials (a newly developed questionnaire and the data sheet) have been transformed into an online application, of course after some adjustments as a result of the pilot. This online application was used to carry out the extended research.

## 6.4.3  Extended Research

The application that was used to carry out the extended research includes statements, and the respondent is asked which statement best fits the companies' product and that of two of their most important competitors. Some examples of these statements are:

☐ The number of parts is relatively high
☐ The number of parts has decreased
☐ The number of parts is at its minimum
☐ The ergonomic demands and the way the product is being handled can be improved
☐ The product is easy to handle and meets the ergonomic demands
☐ The product's styling is of minor concern
☐ The styling of the parts of the product is good

☐ The product's styling is expressive
☐ The provider can distinguish himself by a good but simple and sober design

This application was used to carry out the research, together with 20 companies. The range of products with which the companies took part was divers. The investigated products vary from a small wallet to a windmill and from an umbrella to a hand-soap pump.

The application proved to be an adequate method for determining the product phase of a product. The graphics, which are the result of the online questionnaire answered by the entrepreneur, product manager or designer (Figure 6.4.1), matched the opinion of the researchers. The newly formed innovation strategies have been discussed with the participating companies. In general, most companies were again positive about the results and willing to follow some of the suggestions. However, some companies did have some critics concerning the innovation strategies regarding the promotion of products. In their opinion their products are not suitable for promotion through paid TV and radio advertising.

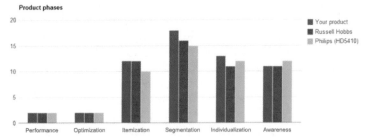

FIGURE 6.4.1
Determination of the product phases of three coffee machines with the aid of the EPRO tool.

To verify that the software application gives the same results as a 'manual advice', an experiment was carried out with students of Industrial Design Engineering at the University of Twente.

In the course of Evolutionary Product Development, the history of a product is studied with Eger's theory of product phases in mind. The literature to be reviewed consists of professional and scientific publications and consumer guides. Copies of relevant articles from the Dutch 'Consumentengids' were provided. In a follow-up course a new design was made for the product. This design has to be a feasible 'next logic step' (of course there are always several possibilities) based on the theory of product phases. This means that the design can never be a 'revolutionary concept', although it can contain new production methods, materials or other state-of-the-art features. The first course ended with a report about the history of the product examined. The analysis needs to include a mapping of the product characteristics based on the six phases (text and table) and a description of how the product changed over time (in terms of dominant design, features, complexity, production methods, perception, legislation etc.). An important deliverable of the course is a short comparison between one of the analyzed products that is now on the market (free to choose) and two competitors. In very short descriptions (one sentence) suggestions have to be given for what the entrepreneur (or the designer) of the chosen product should do with regard to product development based on the 18 aspects described in Section 6.4.2. After the students had compared the product of their choice with two competitive products, and had given their 18 recommendations, they were asked to use the software application.

The results of the application were compared with the student's 'manual' results. The results of 24 of the 28 students who participated in the course could be used. It proved that, in most cases, the manual results show similarities to the computer-generated results. Almost all products were positioned in the same product phase and most innovation strategies were similar.

From the research with the companies and the students it can be concluded that, for a first design, the results are encouraging, although the software application certainly needed improvement. First of all, some descriptions of the tool are not very clear, for example 'The number of parts has to be at its minimum'. This concerns the number of parts necessary to fulfil the basic functionality. Extra features and accessories are excluded. (E.g. the first mobile telephone had a lot of parts that were all necessary for the function of calling. Current mobile phones still have many parts, but very few of those are necessary for the function of making phone calls.)

Second, when companies were asked to choose a tool, some of them said they have plans to enter the market with a (for them) new product. They would like to use the tool to determine the product phase of their competitors and come up with innovation strategies for a new product with a better competitive position. Unfortunately, while using the tool during this research it was not possible to analyze just two competitors.

Third, the tool does not consider the recommendations, but makes suggestions that the students (or an expert) would leave out. For instance, during the pilot the tool suggested that a market leader in highly priced ladders should lower his prices. The product manager considered this a suggestion that the company would most likely not follow because of its status as market leader. The question remains as to whether this really is a problem that has to be solved (e.g. by asking the company about their pricing strategy) or if it is better to let the entrepreneur make his own choices and rather use the suggestions of the application as a checklist (after all, it is a possibility to lower the prices).

## 6.5  Towards the Final Tool and How to Use It

### 6.5.1  Optimization of the Tool

The results of extended research were so promising that the decision was made to repeat the experiment, both with more companies, as in a next year's course. The tool was optimized on the basis of the results of the extended research with the companies, the results of the research with the students and later studies of the model of product phases.

Based on the research with the companies, some extra information was added to ensure a better understanding of the questions. Besides this, the tool is now suitable for companies that do not yet have a product on the market, but that want to start developing once they have found out how to be ahead of their competitors. Based on the research with the students, it is now emphasized that the tool only provides possible solutions and that the entrepreneur or designer will always be the one who has to decide which one to choose.

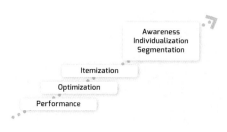

FIGURE 6.5.1
Product phases: the last three phases co-exist.

Besides the optimization based on the research whilst developing and testing the tool, newly gathered insights into the theory of Evolutionary Product Development also led to some changes. According to a recent study (see Chapter 7), the last three phases coexist rather than following one another (Figure 6.5.1). This influences the given innovation strategies when products are already positioned in one of the last phases. In the same study two of the product characteristics proved to be statistically insignificant, namely the number of competitors and promotion. For this reason innovation strategies concerning these characteristics have been eliminated from the tool. Most of the time, both of them are not directed by designers. One of them, the number of competitors, is usually a given fact. The second, the way promotion is achieved, is in most cases not, or only partially, influenced by designers.

## 6.5.2  The New Tool

After carrying out the pilot and the extended research with the 20 companies and the students, a new version of the tool was developed. The optimized questions for determination of the product phases and, subsequently, determination of strategies are as follows:

### 1. Newness
*Your product, Competitor 1, Competitor 2 (All questions have to be answered three times, one time for the product of the user of the tool, two times for the chosen competitors)*

☐ The product is new to the market
☐ The product has a certain – but limited – familiarity within the target group
☐ Almost everybody of the target group owns, knows or has heard of the product

### 2. Functionality and Reliability
*Information: Reliability concerns the quality of a product to fulfil its function under certain circumstances and for a certain period, without failure. When for example the reliability of an electric blanket is three years, this means that the blanket will fulfil its function (heating) without*

*failure, under normal circumstances, for a period of at least three years. If the reliability of competing products is much higher, this may be considered as deficient/moderate.*

*Your product, Competitor 1, Competitor 2*

☐ The product's functionality is deficient/moderate
☐ The product's functionality is reasonable
☐ The product's functionality and reliability are good

### 3. Technology

*Information: Technology push means that the product has been introduced to the market recently and uses a new technology (which is still in development). Some good examples of recent technology push products are a 3D printer or an electric car.*

*Your product, Competitor 1, Competitor 2*

☐ The product is ensued from 'technology push'
☐ The product is not ensued from 'technology push'

### 4. Amount of parts

*Information: This concerns the amount of parts to fulfil the product's basic functionality. Extra features and accessories are excluded, because that often leads to more parts.*
*Your product, Competitor 1, Competitor 2*

☐ The amount of parts is relatively high
☐ The amount of parts decreases
☐ The amount of parts is at its minimum

### 5. Ergonomics
*Your product, Competitor 1, Competitor 2*

☐ The ergonomic demands and the way the product is handled can be improved
☐ The product is easy to handle and meets the ergonomic demands

### 6. Safety

*Information: Note that safety does not necessarily mean injuries, but can also concern computer safety (hacking).*
*Your product, Competitor 1, Competitor 2*

☐ The safety of the product can be improved
☐ The product is safe

### 7. Assortment/Choices
*Your product, Competitor 1, Competitor 2*

☐ The product offers few choices: there is a small assortment
☐ The product offers many choices: the product line is broad

### 8. Ethics
*Attention: several answers are possible*
*Your product, Competitor 1, Competitor 2*

☐ The provider communicates about the ethic targets of the company

- ☐ The provider does not communicate about the ethic targets of the company
- ☐ The social behaviour of the provider is not of major concern for the user's purchasing behaviour
- ☐ The provider can distinguish himself from his competitors by his social behaviour, e.g. in relation to environment, child labour etc.

### 9. Product Development
*Attention: several answers are possible*
*Your product, Competitor 1, Competitor 2*

- ☐ Product development mainly aims at improvement of functionality
- ☐ Product development aims at improvement of functionality and reliability, ergonomics and/or safety
- ☐ Product development aims at development of extra features and/or properties
- ☐ Product development aims at different types of products for different trading channels or target groups
- ☐ Product development aims at creating possibilities for the user to affect the product's functionality by choosing from extra features or to compose his own product

### 10. Styling
*Your product, Competitor 1, Competitor 2*

- ☐ The product's styling is of minor concern
- ☐ The styling of the parts of the product is good
- ☐ The product's styling is expressive

### 11. Form Integration
*Your product, Competitor 1, Competitor 2*

- ☐ Form giving is not very important, matching form giving with different parts of the product is poor
- ☐ The styling of the parts of the product (integration of form) is good

### 12. Number of Competitors/Providers/Manufacturers
*Your product, Competitor 1, Competitor 2*

- ☐ There is just one/are just a few provider(s)/manufacturer(s)
- ☐ There are more (but not many) providers/manufacturers
- ☐ There are many providers, competition is high

### 13. Pricing
*Your product, Competitor 1, Competitor 2*

- ☐ The price of the product is relatively high
- ☐ Competition is based on price
- ☐ The unit price is under pressure because of competition
- ☐ The unit price is at its minimum
- ☐ The unit price can be varied through adjustment of the product to the requirements of the individual user

### 14. Production
*Your product, Competitor 1, Competitor 2*

☐ The product has been designed for manufacturing with standard production facilities
☐ Automation of production gets more important (only of importance when production series allow this)
☐ Production of the product has been automated to a high level (only of importance when production series allow this)
☐ None of the above mentioned answers / Not applicable

## 15. Assembly
*Your product, Competitor 1, Competitor 2*

☐ The product's assembly mainly occurs manually
☐ Assembly of the product is automated to a high level or has been outsourced to low labour countries (only of importance when production series allow this)
☐ None of the above mentioned answers / Not applicable

## 16. Promotion
*Attention: several answers are possible*
*Your product, Competitor 1, Competitor 2*

☐ Promotion occurs through fair participation and free publicity
☐ Promotion is at a small scale: fairs, internet, brochures etc.
☐ Promotion occurs through advertisements in magazines and newspapers and/or on radio and TV
☐ Promotion occurs through direct marketing, interactive media or social media
☐ Marketing is intensive: much advertising in many media
☐ None of the above mentioned answers / Not applicable

## 17. Influence of the Consumer on the Final Product
*Attention: several answers are possible*
*Your product, Competitor 1, Competitor 2*

☐ Interactive media are used to adjust the product to the individual user
☐ The user communicates directly with the provider to clarify his individual wishes
☐ None of the above mentioned answers / Not applicable

## 18. Service
*Your product*

☐ The product does not have an organized service (which does not mean that no service is provided)
☐ The product has a well-developed service organization

### 6.5.3 Using the Tool

The final version of the tool can be used by owners of this book and can be found on www.fever.nl/epro/. Once the link has been clicked, an introduction window appears.

❶ Choose your language (Dutch or English). Press the 'Start enquiry' button after having read the introduction.

❷ Fill in the form with personal information. Press the 'Send' button.

❸ Start the questionnaire. Answer all questions for both your product as well as the products of your competitors.

❹ When a hyperlink appears displaying the text 'more information', some additional information can be found when clicking in this link.

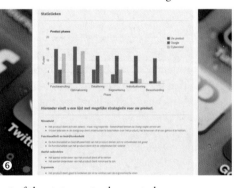

❺ When the circles in front of the statements change to boxes, more than one box can be selected.

⑥ After having finished all 18 questions, the result will be shown in the form of a histogram. The histogram shows the score per product phase for all three products. The highest bar refers to the product phase in which the product best fits at that moment in time. This is the optimization phase for the product of the company for which the questionnaire has been used (blue bar).

⑦ The innovation strategies can be found underneath the graphic. A summary of the answers can be found by scrolling down further.

### 6.5.4 Elaborated Example of a Product for Aquatic Sports

In this section some results of the tool are shown. Note that this is a selection of the total output. Company names and some of the recommendations were left out because of confidentiality.

**Personal information**

| | |
|---|---|
| Name of your organization: | xxxxxxx |
| Line of business: | Aquatic sports |
| Product for which you want to determine the product phase: | Generator set |
| Competitor 1: | Whisperpower |
| Competitor 2: | Fisher Panda |

**Statistics**

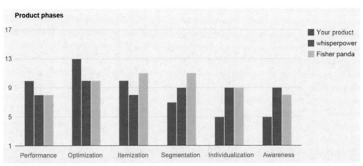

Below you will find a list of possible strategies for your product.

### Number of Parts

- The number of parts should be kept to a minimum, if possible the amount of parts should decrease.

### Ergonomics

- The ergonomics and the user interface of the product can be improved.

### Assortment/Amount of Choices the Product Offers

- The product does not offer much choice, there is room for segmentation.

### Ethics

- The user might become more interested in the companies behaviour with regard to the environment.
- Your company could communicate more about your ethic targets.

### Product Development

- Product development could aim at different types of products for different trading channels or target groups.
- Product development could aim at development of extra features and/or accessories.

### Price

- The unit price will soon be at its minimum. An opportunity may be to vary the unit price by adjustment of the product to the individual user.

### Production

- Automation of production offers possibilities.

### Assembly

- Automation or outsourcing of assembly to low wages countries offer chances.

# 7 RESEARCH PERFORMED TO VERIFY THE THEORY OF EVOLUTIONARY PRODUCT DEVELOPMENT

This chapter summarizes the research that was undertaken in order to show that the product phases exist, whether they appear in the expected order and whether the product characteristics describe the product phases in the correct way. The following questions will be answered:

*Do the described product characteristics appear in the order that is predicted by the product phases?*

*Are the product phases an appropriate means of helping to predict the future of a product based on its history?*

*Do products always (or most of the time) follow the product phases in the predicted sequence?*

*Can a phasing of the life cycle of a product based on the product phases offer designers starting points for a new product development?*

Den Hertog and Van Sluijs (1995) describe the research methods that are available for research into the effectiveness of innovations. They distinguish five groups of methods: experiment, survey, case study, action research and ethnography. For the subject we are interested in, the retrospective case study and the survey are the most suitable.

## 7.1  Study 1: Retrospective Case Survey

A retrospective case study involves the study of many aspects of one case and contrasts with a survey, during which a few aspects of many cases are studied. The study of one case is insufficient for an investigation of the product phases, and five cases seem possible. The number of aspects that have to be studied is much more limited. Therefore, a comparative (multiple) retrospective case survey, a method that lies between the survey and the case study, seems the best choice, as it means that a few cases are studied based on a small number of aspects. Study 1 is therefore based on a retrospective survey of five cases. According to Eisenhardt (1989), between 4 and 10 cases are usually sufficient for most surveys. In her paper Eisenhardt advocates choosing cases that are very different from one another, to gain a better insight into the applicability of the theory.

For this study the history of five products is analyzed in a comparative multiple retrospective case survey. This is done by means of a literature study and with the aid of interviews of people involved with the products, such as directors, marketing managers, product managers and designers. The following products are analyzed: electric shavers, mobile phones, bicycles, working class housing and travelling (for vacations).

The shaver was chosen because it is an example of a durable consumer product that has gone through a long period of product development. It is supposed that emotional benefits are not as important as they are for products like a mobile phone or a bicycle. After all, a shaver is not usually seen by friends and acquaintances as it rarely leaves the confines of a bathroom. The mobile phone was chosen as an example of a product that was developed very quickly over a very short period of time. Moreover, it is a product that attracted a lot of exposure. The bicycle was chosen because it is a product that people usually use for a very long time (often 10 years or more) and because it has had a long history, meaning that it seems likely that the last two product phases, individualization and awareness, played an important part in the development of this product. Working class housing and holidays were selected to show that the theory of product phases is also suited to architecture and services. Although these products are not the prime subject of this study, it is interesting to see whether the theory can be applied to them. The five studies are described in Chapter 4.

## Conclusions

In most cases the chosen products follow the product phases as expected, albeit with some (often minor) disruptions (see Chapter 4). Furthermore, the findings revealed that it was difficult to draw a fine line between the end of one product phase and the beginning of the next, since some product phases overlap one another for long periods of time. However, in a number of cases the last two phases were absent. One explanation might be that the product has not yet reached these phases. Having said that, an important question that sometimes arises is whether a product is actually suited to reaching the product individualization phase. Finally, it proved that the awareness phase can often be found at the corporate level (as in the example of the electric shaver), but very rarely at the product level.

## 7.2  Study 2: Ranking by Experts

A disadvantage of a retrospective case survey is that the cases are analyzed by someone who has to know the theory of product phases. If not, this person cannot judge whether the case studied meets the formulated criteria. This means that there is a risk that the researcher may (unwittingly) fit the results of his research into the theory of product phases. Another disadvantage is that the experts consulted had to rely on their memory.

These problems are addressed in a second study, which used a method that was previously employed by, among others, Ten Klooster (2002). While developing a method to design packaging, Ten Klooster asked experts to rank steps in the design process that he had written on cards. There are several reasons why this method seems very suitable. First, there is no interview, so the researcher cannot influence the results by the way he asks the questions. Secondly, the cards help the subject to memorize aspects that he would not have thought of by himself. Finally, this method allows for the use of experts (from different backgrounds) in order to rank the cards.

This research was carried out in two parts. In the first part, the pilot study involving four subjects, a test was undertaken in order to find out whether the framework of the research would function well if the instructions were clear and if the statements were properly formulated and understandable. The subjects were (assistant) professors of the Industrial Design Engineering courses at the Universities of Delft and Twente. All subjects were familiar with the theory of product phases. In both the pilot study and the main study, statements were printed on stickers. They were collected on the basis of the product characteristics. These collections were offered to the subjects in a changing, random order. The statements within the collections were randomized as well. The subjects were asked to arrange the statements in historical order, and to attach the stickers in the order they expected them to take place (or order of importance) in the product life cycle. It was possible to allow statements to be made simultaneously, or on several different occasions in time. In the pilot study, the subjects were asked about their meaning with regard to the design, the execution and the comprehensibility of the test. Based on their comments, some formulations were adapted and two extra statements were added.

For the main study, subjects were selected from a population of experienced industrial designers, design managers and marketing managers because it was expected that they would have enough knowledge of product life cycles and would therefore be able to work with the statements on product characteristics. The aim was to select a minimum of seventy subjects to enable statistically reliable conclusions to be drawn. Because it would have taken a lot of time to approach these people individually, make appointments with them and then visit them, the approach was modified in an attempt to combine the experiment with the events at which members of the target group would meet. This led to four sessions being organized that generated 64 subjects. Another 7 subjects, all experienced industrial design engineers, were then approached separately, bringing the total number of subjects to 71.

The working method in the main study was as follows. Each subject received, in random order, 10 folders with indications of the contents:

newness, functionality, product development, styling, number of
competitors, pricing, production, promotion, service and ethics. Each
folder contained between 2 and 10 sheets of stickers bearing the following statements.

1   The product is new to the market.
2.  The product is known (but not well known) within the target group.
3.  The product is well known within the target group.
4.  The market penetration of the product is high.
5.  The performance of the product is poor.
6.  The product originates from a 'technology push'.
7.  Comparatively speaking, the product has many parts.
8.  The performance of the product is acceptable.
9.  The performance and reliability of the product are good.
10. The product is easy to handle and meets ergonomic demands.
11. The product is safe.
12. The product offers a lot of choice, and there is a wide range.
13. The user is interested in adaptations of the product to extend the
    product life cycle (instead of discarding the product to buy a newer
    one).
14. The competitor can distinguish himself with 'positive aging': the
    product becomes more attractive to use.
15. The product development is mainly aimed at improving the perfor-
    mance of the product.
16. Product development is aimed at products that have better perfor-
    mance, are easier to handle, and have improved reliability, ergonom-
    ics, and safety.
17. Product development is aimed at extra features and accessories.
18. Product development is aimed at different products for different
    market channels or target groups.
19. Product development is aimed at the possibility for the user to
    influence the result by choosing from extra features or to have the
    product assembled to meet his demands.
20. Styling is not very important.
21. There is not much unity in the styling of the parts of the product.
22. The styling of the parts of the product (integration of form) is good.
23. The styling of the product is expressive.
24. The competitor can distinguish himself with a well cared for design
    that is also simple and sober.
25. There is only one or there are very few competitors.
26. There are several competitors (but not many).
27. There are a lot of competitors, and the market is highly competitive.
28. The price of the product (per unit) is relatively high, and people find
    the product expensive.
29. The pricing of products is competitive.
30. There is a lot of competition, prices are under pressure and are going
    down.
31. Prices have reached their lowest possible level.
32. Prices vary because the products are customized.

33. The product is designed for production with standard machines, such as lathes, and milling-, trimming-, bending-, and welding machines.
34. Assembly of the product is done mainly by hand.
35. The number of parts of the product decreases, and automation becomes more important.
36. Assembly of the product is highly automated.
37. Production is highly automated.
38. Promotion is mainly based on free publicity and trade fairs.
39. Promotion is carried out on a small scale: trade fairs, the internet, brochures with retailers, etc.
40. Promotion is carried out through advertising in magazines and papers, and/or on radio and TV.
41. Promotion is carried out through direct marketing.
42. Promotion activities are intensive: a lot of advertising in many different media.
43. Interactive media are used to attune the product to the wishes of the individual user.
44. The user communicates directly with the competitor to make his individual wishes known.
45. The competitor communicates about the ethics of his company.
46. There is no well-organized service organization. (This does not mean that the service is poor.)
47. There is a well-organized service organization that supports the product.
48. The ethics of the competitor (manufacturer) is not very important for the user's decision.
49. The competitor (manufacturer) can distinguish himself from the competition by its social behaviour, for example with regard to the environment or child labour.

These statements were based on the descriptions of the product phases. Each sheet had a statement printed on it fourteen times. This was done in order to make it clear that it is possible and permitted to affix a sticker more than once. Overall, each subject received 49 sheets, each with 14 stickers, bringing the total number of stickers to 686. In addition to that they received a piece of paper measuring 50 by 73 cm with indications of the time the product is on the market and the market penetration of the products. The subjects were able to affix the stickers to this piece of paper (the 'field of play').

The intention was to have experts judge and arrange the statements, and since the statements were about both product development and marketing, an attempt was made to find experts from both groups. The idea was to have a 50/50 division. This turned out not to be feasible since the selected group consisted of more than twice the number of product designers than marketers. Nevertheless, the expectation was that the knowledge of marketing within the group was adequate as more than half of the subjects said that they were managers as well. Managers in product development are supposed to have at least some knowledge of marketing. The level of education confirmed this: 95% of the subjects had studied at a university or a University of Applied Sciences, as the syllabus is heavily biased towards marketing. It was also the intention to have experienced subjects participate in this study. This was achieved since 56% had more than five years of experience, and 77% more than two years.

Based on the position of the stickers, a decision was made as to which product phase was related to the statement printed on it. Another thing that was indicated is that there are some statements that typify one product phase, others that typify two or three and others that even typify a maximum of four product phases. The following criteria were used to decide whether a statement can significantly be linked to a product phase. If a statement typifies only one product phase and 17% (rounded off upwards) of the stickers were affixed in the column of this phase, this can be called 'coincidence'. (If the stickers had been affixed randomly, this would give the same result.) If a statement typifies one product phase, and 45% of the stickers have been affixed in the column of this product phase, the conclusion will be that the statement is linked significantly to the product phase. If the number of stickers linked to the product phase is greater than (or equals) 36% and is less than 45%, the link will be called a strong indication; if the number is between 28% and 35%, it will be called an indication, etc. Figure 7.2.1 shows an overview of the criteria that were used to decide whether a link is significant, a strong indication, an indication, a weak indication, a coincidence or is denied in connection with statements relating to one, two, three or four product phases.

FIGURE 7.2.1
Overview of the criteria used to decide whether a statement typifies a product phase in a significant number of the cases.

| Number of product phases | Denied | Coincidence | Weak indication | Indication | Strong indication | Significant |
|---|---|---|---|---|---|---|
| 1 | X < 15% | 15 ≤ X ≤ 19 | 20 ≤ X ≤ 27 | 28 ≤ X ≤ 35 | 36 ≤ X ≤ 44 | X ≥ 45% |
| 2 | X < 31% | 31 ≤ X ≤ 35 | 36 ≤ X ≤ 43 | 44 ≤ X ≤ 52 | 53 ≤ X ≤ 61 | X ≥ 62% |
| 3 | X < 48% | 48 ≤ X ≤ 52 | 53 ≤ X ≤ 60 | 61 ≤ X ≤ 68 | 69 ≤ X ≤ 77 | X ≥ 78% |
| 4 | X < 65% | 65 ≤ X ≤ 69 | 70 ≤ X ≤ 77 | 78 ≤ X ≤ 85 | 86 ≤ X ≤ 94 | X ≥ 95% |

The criteria of Figure 7.2.1 were defined as follows. A statement can apply to a maximum of four product phases. Therefore, the situation in which this is the case was examined first. A requirement that 95% of the stickers are affixed to these four product phases seems necessary because, if 'coincidence' were to be the case, 67% of the stickers would already be linked to these phases. Ultimately, however, this requirement proved to be excessive since none of the statements could actually meet it. For each of the lower product phases, the chance of coincidence is reduced by 16.667%. It therefore seems realistic to minimize the criterion of significance by the same steps. In this way the percentages of 45, 62 and 78 were set. Next the difference between the situation of 'coincidence' and 'significant' was divided into three equal steps that were named 'strong indication', 'indication' and 'weak indication'.

Figures 7.2.2 to 7.2.4 provide examples of how the stickers were attached to the 'field of play' for three of the statements.

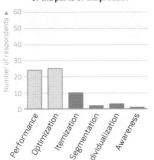

**There is not much unity in the styling of the parts of the product**

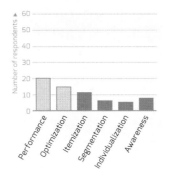

**Styling is not very important**

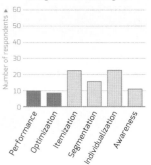

**The styling of the parts of the product (integration of form) is good**

FIGURE 7.2.2
Statement 21, conclusion: significant.
Light green: number of stickers that was applied according to the theory.

FIGURE 7.2.3
Statement 20, conclusion: strong indication.
Light green: number of stickers that was applied according to the theory.

FIGURE 7.2.4
Statement 22, conclusion: indication.
Light green: number of stickers that was applied according to the theory.

## Conclusions

Based on the criteria formulated above, the presumed relationship between a statement and the associated product phases was significant in 17 cases, and in 13 cases there was a strong indication. On 3 occasions there was an indication, on 10 occasions a weak indication, on 5 occasions no evidence of a relationship was found ('coincidence'), and on only 1 occasion was there a result that there was no relationship at all. Based on the classification by the experts, it can be concluded about the 49 statements that they describe the product characteristics and the product phases with mixed results. The first two product phases are described in the range of 'well' to 'very well'. From the statements about the product performance phase, a value of 93% is confirmed by the experts. For the optimization phase this percentage reaches 85. The next four phases are not described so well. Itemization has the lowest score, as only 56% of the statements are confirmed by the experts. The percentage for segmentation is 67, for individualization it is 62% and for awareness it is 57%. It should be noted that the experts deny a statement only once, and that any other statements that are not confirmed are not denied either (Figure 7.2.5).

| Product phase | Number of statements (1) | Number confirmed (2) | Percentage |
|---|---|---|---|
| Performance | 15 | 14 | 93 |
| Optimization | 20 | 17 | 85 |
| Itemization | 16 | 9 | 56 |
| Segmentation | 21 | 14 | 67 |
| Individualization | 21 | 13 | 62 |
| Awareness | 23 | 13 | 57 |

FIGURE 7.2.5
The percentage of the statements that were confirmed by the experts per product phase.
(1) The number of statements that are concerned with this product phase.
(2) The number of statements that were considered by the experts to relate to this product phase.

FIGURE 7.2.6
The percentage of the statements that were confirmed
by the experts per product
characteristic.
(1) The number of statements
that are concerned with this
product characteristic.
(2) The number of state-
ments that were considered
by the experts to be con-
cerned with this product
characteristic.

| Product characteristic | Number of statements (1) | Number confirmed (2) | Percentage |
|---|---|---|---|
| Newness | 10 | 10 | 100 |
| Functionality | 24 | 15 | 63 |
| Product development | 13 | 9 | 69 |
| Styling | 11 | 8 | 73 |
| Number of competitors | 7 | 7 | 100 |
| Pricing | 11 | 7 | 64 |
| Production | 12 | 12 | 100 |
| Promotion | 16 | 4 | 25 |
| Service | 6 | 6 | 100 |
| Ethics | 6 | 2 | 33 |

In general, it can be concluded that the product characteristics pertaining to the product, such as newness, functionality, product development
and form giving, describe the product phases very well. The same can
be said about the product characteristics pertaining to the market (the
number of competitors and price), production and service. According
to the experts, the two remaining product characteristics of 'promotion'
and 'ethics' do not have adequate descriptions to base a conclusion on
(Figure 7.2.6).

## Conclusions per Product Phase

- With the exception of the statement on the social behaviour of the
  competitor (statement 48), it can be concluded that the product
  characteristics describe the product performance phase very well.
- With the exception of the statements on product development
  (statement 16), pricing (statement 29) and the social behaviour of
  the competitor (statement 48), it can be concluded that the product
  characteristics describe the product optimization phase quite well.
- The product characteristics only reasonably describe the product
  itemization phase, and statements regarding the performance of
  the product (10 and 11), product development (16), pricing (29) and
  promotion (40 and 41) give a different picture. What is more, the
  statement about the social behaviour is incorrect, but that is the case
  for all of the product phases.
- The product characteristics describe the product segmentation
  phase in the range of 'reasonable' to 'well'. The statements regarding
  promotion (40, 41 and 42), safety (11), and the styling of the product
  (23) give different results. Once again, the statement about social
  behaviour is incorrect.
- The product characteristics describe the product individualization
  phase with mixed success. The statements concerning performance,
  product development and styling are precarious. The statements
  regarding the newness, the market, the production and the service
  have proved to be correct. The statements regarding the promotion
  and social behaviour of the competitor are, once again, inadequate.
- The product characteristics do not adequately describe the product
  awareness phase. In particular, the characteristics that typify the
  product phase, such as a sober design (statement 24) and the importance of ethics (statements 13 and 45), are hardly recognized by the

subjects. The statements that match this phase are the ones that also match the individualization phase, namely newness, production, service and (only partially) the market.

## 7.3 Study 3: IDE Students' Use of the Model in the Evolutionary Product Development Course

In the previously mentioned studies one question remained unanswered, namely the extent to which designers are able to make 'correct predictions' about future products on the basis of the theory of product phases. The research question addressed in Study 3 is whether the model of product phases can be helpful when predicting the future development of a product. Does the model offer designers starting points when developing new products? Do designers consider these starting points too rigid or does the model leave too much design freedom?

In the next section the following research question will be discussed:

***Find out to what extent designers are able to make 'correct predictions about future products', based on the theory of product phases.***

This main question can be divided into the following sub-questions:
a. Is the model a useful tool in the first phase of the design process, when the product and the market are analyzed?
b. Does it offer starting points for a redesign?
c. Can it give directions regarding functionality or styling of a product?
d. Does it leave enough design freedom for the designer, or do designers consider the starting points too rigid? (See the Conclusions for more detail on the delicate balance between 'enough freedom' and 'too much rigidity'.)

The results presented in this section are based on the work of 81 students of the Master's course in Evolutionary Product Development.[10] These students created new designs for 73 products making use of the model of the product phases. Eight products were worked on twice (Figure 7.3.1). The instructions to the students were to study and analyze the history of a product of their choice, and to create a new design for this product, both by making use of the model. The designs were created in a period between 2005 and 2008. In this period the course was given three times.

---

10 This research is based on the work that was done by students who participated in the Master's course in Evolutionary Product Development. This course is part of the two-year Master's programme in Industrial Design Engineering at the University of Twente. In the first part of the course the history of a chosen product is studied with the theory of product phases in mind. An existing product is analyzed. An example of the product has to be bought and is dismantled during a practical. Special attention has to be paid to the production methods used (forming, separating and joining processes), use of materials, surface textures (coatings) and product arrangement or assemblies. In the second part of the course a redesign is made for the product. This design has to be a possible 'next logic step' (of course, there are always several possibilities) based on the theory of product phases (Eger and Wendrich, 2011).

FIGURE 7.3.1
The 73 products that were
redesigned by Master's
students with the number
of times the product was
chosen shown between
parentheses.

Angle grinder, Back pack (2), Bicycle, Blender, Calculator, Cast away camera,
CD player, Children's bicycle seat, Clock, Coffee grinder, Computer mouse,
Cyclometer, Digital photo frame, Electric cooker, Electric drill (2), Electric fan
heater, Electric guitar, Electric kettle, Electric shaver (2), Electric toothbrush
(2), Espresso machine (2), Facial tanner, Food processor, Fountain pen, Game
controller, Glasses (2), Hair dryer, Hand mixer, Hand vacuum cleaner, Hockey
stick, Iron, Ironing table, Jigsaw, Juicer, Kettle, Keyboard, Kitchen scales, Kitchen
timer, Knijpkat (hand powered flashlight), Ladyshave, Mechanical alarm clock,
Microphone, Mobile phone, Moped, MP3 player, PC, Perforator, Radio, Receiver,
Record player, Sail board, Sanding machine, Scales, Skis, Speaker box, Stereo
amplifier, Table fan, Table lamp, Telephone, Tennis racquet, Tent, TIG welding
torch, Toaster (2), Toy cars, TV, Vacuum cleaner, Vacuum flask, Walkie talkie,
Walkman/MP3 player, Wall socket, Watch, Webcam, Wet shavers (2)

The courses resulted in 81 tables, and an example of such a table is given
in Figure 7.3.2. Based on this data an assessment was made regarding the
level at which the analyzed products fulfil the theory of product phases
and which of the product characteristics best describe the product
phases.

FIGURE 7.3.2
Example of a table that
illustrates the extent to
which a product applies to
the theory of product phases. The six product phases
are shown horizontally, and
the 10 product characteristics vertically.
+ = applies;
– = does not apply;
+/– = applies only partially;
? = unknown, uncertain.

| Product characteristic | Performance | Optimization | Itemization | Segmentation | Individualization | Awareness |
|---|---|---|---|---|---|---|
| Newness | + | + | + | + | + | + |
| Functionality | + | + | + | + | + | + |
| Product development | + | + | + | + | + | + |
| Styling | + | + | + | + | + | + |
| Number of competitors | – | – | – | + | + | + |
| Pricing | + | + | + | + | + | + |
| Production | ? | ? | ? | ? | ? | ? |
| Promotion | +/– | +/– | + | + | + | + |
| Service | + | + | + | + | + | + |
| Ethics | + | + | + | + | + | + |

The following argumentation was used for the statistical verification
of the results. In principle, the possible answers to each question either
consist of 'does apply/true' (=1), or 'does not apply/false' (=0). It can
therefore be stated that there is a binominal distribution with a test
hypothesis of pi = 0.5. Because the number of observations is 81, this
distribution can be addressed with a standard normal distribution. The
results from the tables (Figure 7.3.2) were interpreted as follows: Only
the characteristics that scored with a '+' were considered to be 'true'.
All other possibilities – '+/–', '–' and '?' – were indicated as 'false', thus
introducing an element of counter-biasing to the processing of the data.
The results can be found in Figure 7.3.3. It should be noted that, of the
researched products, 21 products had reached the individualization
product phase, and only 8 had reached the awareness phase. The data
from these two phases therefore only provide an indication and cannot
be regarded as statistically significant.

| Product characteristic | Performance | Optimization | Itemization | Segmentation | Individualization | Awareness |
|---|---|---|---|---|---|---|
| **Total** | **1.78** | **1.65** | **2.25** | **3.5** | **3.11** | **1.89** |
| **Number of observations** | 81 | 81 | 81 | 80 | 21 | 8 |
| Newness | 2.35 | 0.8 | 0.81 | 4.36 | 4.4 | 4.4 |
| Functionality | 2.9 | 1.8 | 4.4 | 2.42 | 4.4 | 4.4 |
| Product development | 4.4 | 2.44 | 2.44 | 3.0 | 1.0 | 0.33 |
| Styling | 1.71 | 0.48 | 1.62 | 1.8 | 2.07 | 1.17 |
| Number of competitors | 1.47 | 0.64 | 0.24 | 1.12 | 0.73 | 0.63 |
| Pricing | 1.48 | 1.18 | 1.14 | 1.55 | 2.07 | 0.63 |
| Production | 2.81 | 1.0 | 0.77 | 0.69 | 0.35 | 1.17 |
| Promotion | 1.43 | 0.39 | 0.41 | 0.04 | -0.46 | -0.33 |
| Service | 1.03 | 0.61 | 0.92 | 1.54 | 2.07 | 4.4 |
| Ethics | 4.09 | 2.92 | 4.18 | 1.74 | -0.56 | -0.33 |

| 3.09 | Significant at 1% level | 1.65 | Significant at 5% level |
|---|---|---|---|
| 1.97 | Significant at 2,5% level | < 1.645 | Not significant |

To illustrate the students' results, four designs were selected. The first three examples show how the theory can give direction to the design process. The fourth project provides an example of how and why 3 of the 81 students decided to deviate from the model. The examples were also chosen because they provide an example of products in the product phases that most of the students concluded their product could be found: segmentation, individualization and awareness (Eger & Drukker, 2012).

## Example 1: Moped
*Student: Victor van Eekelen*

Van Eekelen determined that the moped is in the individualization phase. It is possible to have a moped custom made to a great extent (mass customization), and there are many accessories on the market that people can assemble themselves. He also concluded that the market in the Netherlands consists mainly of young people aged between 16 and 18, who are not very sensitive to the ethical aspects of the mopeds or their manufacturers. He therefore chose to try to design a moped that can be positioned in the awareness phase, aimed at a somewhat older target group, but styled in a way that the moped is also attractive for younger people. He chose this design direction because he believed that there are no mopeds aimed at this target group. Aspects he added to his design that should make his product attractive for this group are an economical four-stroke engine, an exhaust pipe with attenuation and filters, and steel parts because they are stronger, easier to repair and more suitable for recycling (Figure 7.3.4).

FIGURE 7.3.4
Redesign of a moped in the awareness phase by Victor van Eekelen (2005).

## Example 2: Bicycle
*Student: Koen van der Wal*

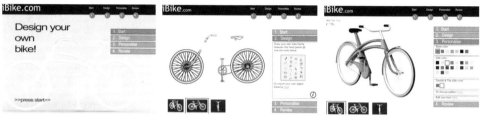

FIGURE 7.3.5
Website to design your own
bicycle (individualization
phase) by Koen van der Wal
(2005).

Van der Wal believes the bicycle to be in both the individualization phase and the awareness phase. Since halfway through the 1980s it has been possible to have your own bicycle custom built. Bicycles entered the awareness phase somewhere around 1980, but for slightly different reasons than the theory of product phases predicts. In this period the bicycle was rediscovered as a healthy and environmentally friendly alternative to the 'unhealthy and polluting' car. However, these qualities were not deliberately developed by manufacturers, for instance by using environmentally friendly materials and production processes or by committing themselves to social responsibility. These qualities were simply inherent in the product itself and would have come to the surface anyway, even if manufacturers had had no environmental conscience at all. Van der Wal chose to investigate the individualization phase in more detail because he saw opportunities for an interactive website that would make it possible for consumers to design their own bicycle. His website offers consumers a number of fixed positions (saddle, handlebar, crankshaft and front crutch) between which they can design their own frame. Examples of pages of his website can be found in Figure 7.3.5.

## Example 3: Toaster
*Student: Ruud Elders*

FIGURE 7.3.6
Redesign of a toaster in the
segmentation phase by Ruud
Elders (2006).

According to Elders, the toaster is in the segmentation phase, and he argues that it is very likely that the product will stay there. According to him, the need to individualize the product is non-existent. The simplicity and long product life do not offer many chances for a design aimed at the awareness phase. He therefore chose a target group that he described using the following key words: young, single, trendy, dynamic, hurried, career-oriented. With regard to the use moment he chose breakfast. This target group means the toaster ought to be suitable for new and bigger kinds of bread, with thicknesses of up to one inch. His design is depicted in Figure 7.3.6.


## Example 4: Clock
*Student: Vincent Geraedts*

FIGURE 7.3.7
Redesign of a clock in the awareness phase by Vincent Geraedts (2006).

The segmentation of the clock is such – there is so much choice – that, according to Geraedts, there is no need for individualization.

Time is very important [...] The 24 hours economy runs at full speed [...] Time is dominant [...] The consequence is that time dictates peoples' lives [...] A half hour of extra time is sometimes considered a precious gift.

He therefore chose to make his design of a clock a statement on how time rules our lives. His design, called 'Tea-time', is a clock that 'does not want to be a clock'. The cup and saucer of the clock form the hour- and minute-hands of the clock. When using the clock, by drinking tea from one of the 'hands', time is, so to speak, brought to a standstill (Figure 7.3.7).


## Conclusions

Master's students who participated in the Evolutionary Product Development course were very competent when it came to developing a new version of an existing product. They all used the model, and most of them found good starting points, both in the theory and in what their research into the history of the product produced. Remarkably the students nearly all chose consumer products (BtoC) and – according to their research – the products were all in the segmentation phase or in one of the two subsequent phases (Figure 7.3.8). The only BtoB product that was chosen was the TIG welding torch, which, according to the researcher, was in the itemization phase. In only three cases did the students decide not to follow the theory. One of these cases can be found in the previous section, namely the clock. The other two were the facial tanner and the pocket calculator. Research into the history of the product proved that the facial tanner was at the end of its economic life cycle. The student therefore decided to develop a new product (in the performance phase) aimed as much as possible at the same target group. In the second example it was proven that a calculator function nowadays can be found in a lot of products, such as mobile phones, PDAS, and laptops. The pocket calculator is only still used as a present

| | |
|---|---|
| Performance | 0 |
| Optimization | 0 |
| Itemization | 1 |
| Segmentation | 63 |
| Individualization | 12 |
| Awareness | 5 |
| **Total** | **81** |

FIGURE 7.3.8
Present product phase of the researched products according to the master students.

| | |
|---|---|
| Performance | 2 |
| Optimisation | 0 |
| Itemisation | 0 |
| Segmentation | 80 |
| Individualisation | 51 |
| Awareness | 54 |

FIGURE 7.3.9
Product phases considered by the students for the redesign of the chosen product.

FIGURE 7.3.10
The road map used in the Bachelor's course at the University of Twente. The road map consists of four steps: preliminary phase, design phase, embodiment and detailing phase and implementation phase. (Source: Eger et al., 2013)

given to business acquaintances. On the basis of this finding the student decided to make use of a completely new technique for his calculator, namely the micro liquid technique. He also chose for the performance phase (Figure 7.3.9).

In general, it can be concluded that the theory offers a useful tool at the beginning of a new product development project such as during the analysis phase (Figure 7.3.10), where existing, competing products are studied with regard to their functionality, ergonomics, safety and marketing, and in the phase where ideas are generated for the preliminary design. On the other hand, the theory always offers several options, never only one, and these options are not very detailed, leaving a lot of room for the designer to choose and detail the chosen concept. The question is whether it is desirable to offer more detail or whether the remaining design freedom is beneficial to the model. It is perfectly possible that this will differ according to the individual.

## Bottlenecks for the Students

Some of the students used the theory too rigidly. If the theory predicts that the next step is individualization, they decided that the new product had to be positioned in this phase without critically considering whether the product offers enough possibilities to do so, and whether there is a target group that is interested in the proposed concept.

The course assignment stated that the students were supposed to take a small, evolutionary step in their design process. A small number of the students had problems with this part of the assignment and tried to make a revolutionary leap, for instance by choosing a completely new technique or completely new materials. Some students, who had chosen a product in the segmentation phase, had doubts as to whether the product would ever reach one of the next phases. Their considerations, written down in their reports, contributed to the conclusion that the last three phases often coexist, as described in Chapter 3. Figure 7.3.11 gives an overview of the phases the products were in according to the students, and the phases in which the students' redesign was positioned.

| Present product phase | No. | Product phase chosen for redesign |
|---|---|---|
| | 1 | **Segmentation** |
| **Itemization** | 0 | **Individualization** |
| | 0 | **Awareness** |
| | 2 | **Performance** |
| | 42 | **Segmentation** |
| **Segmentation** | 16 | **Individualization** |
| | 3 | **Awareness** |
| | 4 | **Segmentation** |
| **Individualization** | 4 | **Individualization** |
| | 4 | **Awareness** |
| | 3 | **Segmentation** |
| **Awareness** | 2 | **Individualization** |
| | 0 | **Awareness** |

FIGURE 7.3.11
Product phases chosen by the students for the redesign. Left column: Present product phase of the analysed product. Right column: Product phase that was chosen. Middle column: No = Number of times the product phase mentioned in the right column was chosen.

## 7.4 Discussion

From the studies (Figure 7.4.1 provides an overview of the results of the three studies) it can be concluded that the product phases are a useful way of describing the historic development of a product and that, in most cases, the product phases appear in the predicted order. In this section, some seemingly conflicting findings are discussed, and the predicting value of the theory is analyzed.

| | Restrospective case survey | Classification by experts | Case studies by master students |
|---|---|---|---|
| Performance | 84 | 93 | 83 |
| Optimization | 76 | 85 | 82 |
| Itemization | 84 | 56 | 85 |
| Segmentation | 88 | 67 | 90 |
| Individualization | 85 | 62 | 85 |
| Awareness | 83 | 57 | 86 |

FIGURE 7.4.1
Percentage of the product characteristics that match the product phases in the retrospective case survey (Chapter 4 and Section 7.1), percentage of the statements that were confirmed by the experts per product phase (Section 7.2) and the percentage of the product characteristics that match the product phases in the research with IDE students (Section 7.3).

Baudet (1986) states that products usually start as 'status products'. Rogers (1995) also mentions status as a motive for people to be the first to purchase a new, innovative product. These statements seem to conflict with the theory of product phases because their status seems to become important only in the product segmentation phase. However, Baudet adds to his statement that these products often 'function poorly compared with existing products, but are wanted despite of that'. As an example he mentions, amongst others, the first cars that were much less reliable than horse-drawn coaches, which were the norm at the time. By doing so he explains the difference between the status aspect in the first product phases and in the product segmentation phase (and the phases thereafter). During the first phases the possession of the product is discriminating (whether the product performs well or not), with no activity by the designer being needed to achieve that. During the latter product phases this is no longer the case and the designer has to add this property (emotional benefit) to his design deliberately.

When looking for a starting point of the product phases in relation to a product it is best not to go much further back in history than the start of the Industrial Revolution (in the second part of the eighteenth century). Although some examples of serial or mass production can be found earlier on in history, it can be concluded that the most important influence of mass production on products and the market started in that period and has gained influence ever since. For most products it is difficult to decide when a product goes from one phase to the next. Generally speaking, the transition from one phase to the next is gradual. Sometimes the product phases overlap for longer periods. For the use of the model this is usually not a big problem. If the model is used as a tool to analyse the history of a product, a period of coexistence can be defined with a start and an end date. If the model is used as a design tool, the next step can be based on one or more of the product characteristics instead of the complete product phase.

In every product phase it is possible to accomplish a technical product advantage with respect to the competition. However, in the later phases it becomes more difficult to find and realize substantial technical improvements.

In the case of some products, such as the wristwatch and the electric shaver, products for women and men are available at a very early stage of the development. It seems obvious to call this segmentation. However, with regard to the other product characteristics, these products do not match the product phase segmentation. The reason for this is that one should speak of product-market combinations instead of products. Generally speaking, men will not choose a women's watch, which means that a women's watch is not part of their product-market combination. The solution is to consider the women's and men's watches as separate products (in the meaning of product-market combinations).

Many products are styled in the dominant style of their time, for instance Art Nouveau or Art Deco. In some cases this may resemble segmentation. However, most of the time this is not the case. Only if the style is used in a different time, such as in retro-design, can the product be considered to be in the segmentation phase.

In Chapters 4 and 7 some remarks were made regarding the theory of product phases. The first phases have been defined with more accuracy than the latter. It seems that the 'career' of a product varies considerably as time progresses. It may be that there is an analogy between the career of a human being and that of a product. It was demonstrated that external factors can disturb the development of the product phases (see also Chapter 6). It also turned out to be difficult to draw a fine line between two different, successive product phases, as product phases can coexist. Despite these limitations, the theory of product phases has proven to be a useful thinking aid that can be used to make the large variation in 'product careers' well-structured and unambiguous.

## Discussion per Product Phase: Optimization, Itemization and Segmentation

According to the theory, the number of product parts decreases from the optimization phase onwards. In their research several students noticed that the number of parts grows instead of decreasing. A possible explanation for this can be found in another product characteristic of the itemization and segmentation phases: 'An endeavour sets in to develop extra features and accessories, including special editions of the product that are developed for different trade channels and target groups'. Adding features and accessories often leads to a more complex product with more parts. A good example of this is the mobile phone. Because of all its extra features, such as music, internet, a camera, GPS, a diary and an address book, it has become much more complicated. A better formulation of this characteristic would be that the basic function (without the extras) can be realized with fewer parts.

Something similar can be concluded with regard to the price of the products. The model predicts that the prices will drop, but that only applies if the products fulfil the basic functions. Products with a lot of extra features usually become more expensive. Often these features are added to make a higher price possible.

## Three Product Phases Simultaneously

The last three product phases – segmentation, individualization and awareness – often coexist. A good example of this phenomenon can be found in the fashion world. Over 3,000 fashion brands currently exist in Western countries. Each of them launches new collections onto the market, sometimes twice a year, sometimes four times and, in the case of some brands, even more often. As a consequence, the chances are very small that you will meet someone wearing the same clothes. Moreover, consumers can create their own combinations. Therefore the need to individualize clothing is not that strong for most consumers. In addition, it has been possible, for a long time now, to have your clothes custom made. The fashion brand 50/50 was successfully introduced in the Netherlands in 2003. Clothing, collected by the Salvation Army, was reused and redecorated and brought to the market 'as new' – a good example of the product phase awareness. It can therefore be concluded that the last three phases coexist in this sector.

There are also products and markets in which there are hardly any possibilities to further segment or individualize a product. Companies in these sectors do not have much choice and often choose the awareness phase. Oil companies are a good example. Most gasoline stations offer five kinds of fuel, namely two types of gasoline, two types of diesel and LPG (Liquified Petroleum Gas). Adding an extra product to this assortment is almost entirely impossible. All gasoline stations would have to install an extra pump and extra facilities to be able to offer the product. This would require huge investments, and it is very questionable whether consumers are interested in this extra choice. The next option would be individualization: The possibility of mixing one's own fuel at the petrol station. A concept like that will be fraught with problems. First, the investment in special equipment to mix the fuels at the station; secondly to find an advantage that the consumer will understand and appreciate and finally, the consumer must be convinced to gather the necessary knowledge to carry out the necessary activities. The chances of such an innovation being successful seem small. It is therefore no coincidence that a lot of oil companies pay attention to environmental problems and communicate about them. Examples are the problems experienced by BP and the Shell advertising campaigns (see Figures 7.4.2 and 7.4.3). To encourage consumers to choose their fuel, oil companies in the Netherlands initiated savings systems (with cards or stamps) and built shops and coffee corners in their stations.

FIGURE 7.4.2
The risk of profiling a company in the awareness phase was shown after the BP ('Beyond Petrol') Gulf of Mexico oil spill on 20 April 2010.

**BP: Gasoline station owners in the USA want to see the BP logo removed from their station**
Vandalism and a decreasing turnover of several dozen per cent are causing American gasoline station owners serious problems. According to the British journal Sunday Telegraph they want to remove the name BP from their stations, sooner rather than later and consider the re-introduction of the Amoco brand. According to the Sunday Times some owners have lost 40% of their turnover. The number of cases of vandalism is also increasing. This is not only the case in the USA, but also in the UK. In London, members of Greenpeace recently blocked 35 of the capital's BP petrol stations.
(*Het Financieele Dagblad, 2 August 2010*)

## Discussion per Product Characteristic

FIGURE 7.4.3
Example of an advertisement by Shell on environmental issues.

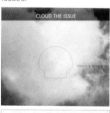

The 'number of competitors' product characteristic proved to be insignificant in all six product phases (Study 3). Because this is a characteristic that does not offer designer starting points for product development, the suggestion is to no longer take this characteristic into consideration when analyzing a product with regard to the product phases.

The 'promotion' product characteristic is also insignificant in all cases (Study 3). The model predicts that promotion shifts from personal and small-scale (fairs, brochures) to impersonal and elaborate (radio, TV, newspapers, magazines). All too often this is not the case. Sometimes TV advertising can be found in the optimization phase and, in other cases, hardly any promotional activities are performed in the segmentation product phase. This applies, for instance, to products that companies add to their portfolio so that they can offer a complete range, even though they know the product will not add much (or even nothing at all) to their profits. An example is the manufacturer of electric drills and sanding machines that added an angle grinder to its range. The question remains as to whether this product characteristic should also be omitted, or whether a better description of the product characteristic is possible.

In Chapter 3 of this publication the product characteristics 'number of competitors' and 'promotion' have not been considered for the reasons mentioned above.

# REFERENCES

ACEA. (2009). Average car age in the EU. Retrieved 17 November 2010 from <www.acea.be/images/uploads/files/20090529_average_car_age.pdf>.

Ames, J.H. & Ames, F.J. (1964). *Improvements in or relating to children's safety seats for use in vehicles and crafts.* The Patent Office.

Anonymous. (1997, January 11). Mobile phones. *Design Engineering.* London.

Anonymous. (2001). *Digitaal Museum van de Volkshuisvesting.* Retrieved 2 June 2008 from <www.iisg.nl/volkshuisvesting/index.html>.

Anonymous. (2004). *Mobile 2003.* Retrieved from <www.motorola.com/MotoInfo>.

Anonymous. (2005a). *Retrobrick – The home of vintage and rare mobile phones.* Retrieved from <www.retrobrick.com/moto8000.html>.

Anonymous. (2005b). *The history of Nokia 1865-2002.* Retrieved from <www.nokia.com/nokiahistory/toimialat/print_tietoliikenne.html>.

ANEC. (2003, *February*). Ronald Vroman (Consumentenbond), Peter Gloyns (VSC), James Roberts (VSC). *Testing of rear seat strength in cars.* Retrieved 14 November 2010 from <www.anec.org/attachments/tr005-03(pictures).pdf>.

ANEC. (2006). *ANEC position on UNECE Regulation 44: Requirements for child restraint systems.* Retrieved 14 November 2010 from <www.anec.org/attachments/ANEC-TRAF-2006-G-040.pdf>.

ANEC. (2011). *I-size: Better protection of children's lives.* Retrieved 25 November 2010 from <www.anec.org/attachments/ANEC-PR-2011-PRL-026.pdf>.

ANEC. (2012). *One-pager on a new regulation on child-restraint systems (the "I- size Regulation").* Retrieved April 5, 2013 from <www.anec.eu/attachments/ANEC-TRAF-2012-G-034.pdf>

Ansoff, H.I. (1965). *Corporate strategy: An analytic approach to business policy for growth and expansion.* New York, NY: McGraw-Hill.

Badke-Schaub, P. (2007). Creativity and innovation in industrial design: Wishful thinking? *Journal of Design Research, 5*(3), 353–367.

Basalla, G. (1988). *The evolution of technology.* Cambridge University Press.

Baudet, H. (1986). *Een vertrouwde wereld; 100 jaar innovatie in Nederland.* Amsterdam: Bert Bakker.

Bense, M. (1954). *Aesthetica, Metaphysische Beobachtungen am Schönen.* Stuttgart: Deutsche Verlags-Anstalt.

Berlyne, D.E. (1971). *Aesthetics and psychobiology.* New York, NY: Appleton-Century-Crofts.

Bijker, W.E. (1990). *The social construction of technology.* Enschede: University of Twente.

Birkhoff, G.D. (1928). Quelques éléments mathématiques de l'art. *Atti del Congresso Internazionale dei Matematci di Bologna.*

Boselie, F.A.J.M. (1982). *Over Visuele Schoonheidservaring.* Nijmegen: Katholieke Universiteit Nijmegen.

Buijs, J. & Valkenburg, R. (2000). *Integrale Productontwikkeling* (2nd fully rev. ed.). Utrecht: Lemma.

Candi, M., Gemser, G. & van den Ende, J. (2010). *Effectiviteit van Design.* Rotterdam: RSM, Erasmus University.

Carlson, W.B. (2000). Invention and evolution: The case of Edison's sketches of the telephone. In J. Ziman (Ed.), *Technological innovation as an evolutionary process.* Cambridge, UK: Cambridge University Press

Christensen, C.M. (1997). *The innovator's dilemma.* Boston, MA: Harvard Business School Press.

Coates, D. (2003). *Watches tell more than time: Product design, information and the quest for elegance.* London, UK: McGraw-Hill.

Colella, J. (2010). *Safe ride news, thirty 'dynamic' years of FMVSS 213.* Retrieved 7 November 2010 from <www.saferidenews.com/SRNDNN/CPSTsProfessionals/HistoryofChildPassengerSafety/ThirtyDynamicYearsofFMVSS213/tabid/249/Default.aspx>.

Consumentengids. (1970). Autozitjes en autogordels, voor kleine kinderen. *Consumentengids,* **18**(5), 148-153.

Consumentengids. (1974). Kinderzitjes en -gordels in de auto. *Consumentengids,* **25**(5), 242-245.

Consumentengids. (1977). Het kind in de auto. Reiswieggordels, zitjes en gordels. *Consumentengids,* **25**(4), 140-147.

Consumentengids. (1983). Zitjes en kussens veilig en prettigst voor uw kind. Kinderbeveiliging in de auto. *Consumentengids,* **31**(8), 358-361.

Consumentengids. (1984). Kinderzitje schiet soms doel voorbij. *Consumentengids,* **32**(6), 268-270.

Consumentengids. (1987). Nu ook een goed zitje voor de allerjongsten. *Consumentengids,* **35**(6), 304-306.

Consumentengids. (1990). Kind in autozitje niet altijd goed beschermd. *Consumentengids,* 38(6), 344-347.

Consumentengids. (1993). *Veel kinderzitjes passen slecht in moderne auto.* Consumentengids, **41**(10), 566-569.

Consumentengids. (1994). Kinderzitjes in auto veiliger. *Consumentengids,* **42**(6), 373.

Consumentengids. (2010). Test autokinderzitje. Maxi-Cosi domineert. *Consumentengids,* **58**(6), 68-71.

Crilly, N., Moultrie, J. & Clarkson, J. (2004). Seeing things: Consumer response to the visual domain in product design. *Design Studies,* **25**, 547-577.

Daniel, E., Wilson, H. & Myers, A. (2008). *Innovation in small and medium sized enterprises.* UK: Cranfield University Press.

Dawkins, R. (1986). *The blind watchmaker.* New York, NY: W.W. Norton & Company.

De Haan, B. & van der Vliet, G. (2005). *Doordouwers en verhalenbouwers.* Enschede: SIR.

De Jong, J.P.J. (2004). *Innovatie in het MKB – Ontwikkelingen sinds 1999.* Zoetermeer: EIM onderzoek voor bedrijf en beleid.

De Meyer, R. & Smets, M. (1982). De recente stedenbouwkundige geschiedschrijving in België omtrent negentiende en begin twintigste eeuw. *Belgisch Tijdschrift voor Nieuwste Geschiedenis,* XIII, 2-3.

De Pauw, G. (Ed.). (2006). De productie van Sociale Woningen. *Art. 23, 22.* Brussels: BBRoW.

Deloitte Research. (2004). *Mastering innovation: Exploiting ideas for profitable growth.* New York, NY: Deloitte Consulting.

Den Hertog, F. & van Sluijs, E. (1995). *Onderzoek in organisaties.* Assen: Van Gorcum.

Desmet, P. (2003). A multilayered model of product emotions. *The Design Journal,* **6**(2), 4-13.

Didde, R. (2004, February 19). Nieuw leven voor elk mobieltje. *De Volkskrant, Bijlage Economie.*

Dijkstra, W. (2005). *De ontwikkeling van het scheerapparaat.* Unpublished master thesis, University of Twente, Enschede.

Dorel. (2005). *Around the world with Maxi-Cosi.* Dorel Netherlands.

The Economist. (1848, 13 May), VI, 536; as cited in Tarn (1973).

Eger, A.O. (1987). Who actually designs? In G. Staal, *Holland in Vorm, Dutch design 1945-1987* (pp. 69-75). The Hague: Stichting Holland in Vorm.

Eger, A.O. (1993). Productniveaus bepalend voor vormgeving, promotie en presentatie (Pt. 1 and 2). *NieuwsTribune,* 47, 32-35 and 48, 27-32.

Eger, A.O. (1996). *Succesvolle Productontwikkeling.* Deventer: Kluwer Bedrijfswetenschappen.

Eger, A.O. (2007). Evolutionary product development: How 'product phases' can map the status quo and future of a product. The Hague: Lemma.

Eger, A.O. (2009). Evolutionary product development in working-class housing. In Liber Amicorum Richard Foqué, *Comparative methodologies: Bringing the world into culture* (pp. 298-317). Antwerp: University Press Antwerp (UPA Editions).

Eger, A.O., Bonnema, G.M., Lutters, E. & van der Voort, M.C. (2013). *Product design.* The Hague: Eleven International Publishing.

Eger, A.O. & Drukker, J.W. (2010). Phases of product development: A qualitative complement to the product life cycle. *Design Issues,* **26**(2), 47-58.

Eger, A.O. & Drukker, J.W. (2012). Evolutionary product development as a design tool. *Journal of Design Research,* **10**(3), 141-154.

Eger, A.O. & Wendrich, R.E. (2011). Knowledge exchange between master and PhD students with regard to evolutionary product development. *Proceedings of the 13th International Conference on Engineering and Product Design Education.* City University (London); 8-9 September 2011; London: The Design Society.

Ehlhardt, H. (1995). *Comfort air, multi-functional air treatment appliances.* Unpublished master thesis, Delft University of Technology.

Eisenhardt, K.M. (1989). Building theories from case study research. *The Academy of Management Review,* **14**(4), 532-550.

Elders, R.G. (2006). *De ontwikkeling van de toaster – productfasen.* Unpublished master thesis, University of Twente, Enschede.

Elkington, J. & Hailes, J. (1992). *Holidays that don't cost the earth.* Londen: Victor Gollancz.

Foot, D.K. (1996). *Boom, bust & echo.* Toronto, Canada: Macfarlane Walter & Ross.

Forty, A. (1986). *Objects of desire.* New York, NY: Thames and Hudson.

Freeman, C. & Louçã, F. (2001). *As time goes by: From the Industrial Revolutions to the Information Revolution.* Oxford: Oxford University Press.

Gaulin, S.J.C. & McBurney, D.H. (2004). *Evolutionary psychology* (2nd ed.). Upper Saddle River, NJ: Prentice Hall.

Geraedts, V.P.J. (2006). *De Klok.* Unpublished master thesis, University of Twente, Enschede.

Hansard. (1851, April, new series). CXV, 1260-1261; as cited in Tarn (1973).

Hekkert, P.P.M. (1995). *Artful judgements.* Delft: TU Delft.

Hoogema, R., Kemp, R., Schot, J. & Truffer, N. (2002). *Experimenting for sustainable transport. The approach of strategic niche management.* London: Spon Press, Taylor & Francis Group.

Joore, P. (2010). *New to improve. The mutual influence between new products and societal change processes.* Delft: VSSD.

Jordan, P.W. (2000). *Designing pleasurable products, an introduction to the new human factors.* London: Taylor & Francis.

Karjaluoto, H. (2005). Factors affecting consumer choice of mobile phones: Two studies from Finland. *Journal of Euromarketing,* **14**(3), 59-82.

Klomp, L. & Van Leeuwen, G. (1999). *The importance of innovation for firm performance.* Voorburg: CBS.

Korbijn, A. (1999). *Vernieuwing in productontwikkeling – Strategie voor de toekomst.* Den Haag: Stichting Toekomstbeeld der Techniek.

Krishnan, V. & Ulrich, K.T. (2001). Product development decisions: A review of the literature. *Management Science,* **47**, 1-21.

Loewy, R. (2011). *Raymond Loewy, the father of industrial design. Retrieved* 30 August 2011 from <www.raymondloewy.com>.

Marzano, S. (2005). *Past tense, future sense.* Amsterdam: BIS.

Maslow, A.H. (1976). *Motivatie en Persoonlijkheid.* Rotterdam: Lemniscaat. (Translation, original edition: Motivation and Personality, 1954)

McDonald Dunbar, R.I. & Knight, C.D. (1999). *The evolution of culture: An interdisciplinary view.* Edinburgh: Edinburgh University Press.

Mitchell, A. (1983). *The nine American life-styles; who we are and where we're going.* New York, NY: Macmillan.

Monö, R. (1997). *Design for product understanding.* Stockholm, Sweden: Liber.

Motivaction Research & Strategy. (2011). *Mentality. Retrieved* July 2011 *from* <www.motivaction.nl/specialismen/mentality-tm>.

Nelson, R.R. & Winter, S.G. (1982). *An evolutionary theory of economic change.* Cambridge, MA: Belknap Press of Harvard University Press.

Norman, D. (1988). *The psychology of everyday things.* New York, NY.

Norman, D. (1992). *Turn signals are the facial expressions of automobiles.* Reading, MA.

Ormerod, P.A. (1994). *The death of economics.* London: Faber and Faber.

Ormerod, P.A. (1998). *Butterfly economics: A new general theory of social and economic behaviour.* London: Faber and Faber.

Ormerod, P.A. (2005). *Why most things fall: Evolution, extinction and economics.* London: Faber and Faber.

Petroski, H. (1992). *The evolution of useful things.* New York, NY: A. Knopf.

The Phrase Finder. (2011). *Beauty is in the eye of the beholder.* Retrieved 19 July 2011 from <www.phrases.org.uk/meanings/59100.html>.

Pine, B.J. & Gilmore, J.H. (1999). *The experience economy*. Boston, MA: Harvard Business School Press.

Popper, K. (1957). *The poverty of historicism*. London: Routledge.

Prahalad, C.K. & Ramaswamy, V. (2004). *The future of competition: Co-creating value with customers*. Boston, MA: Harvard Business School Press.

Pullen, A., De Weerd-Nederhof, P., Groen, A., Song, M. & Fisscher, O. (2009). Successful patterns of internal SME characteristics leading to high overall innovation performance. *Creativity and Innovation Management*, **18**, 209-223.

Ramakers, R. (1984). Van sigaar naar pijp en verder. *Vorm & industrie in Nederland 1: huishoudelijke artikelen*. Rotterdam: Uitgeverij 010.

Rietveld, J. & Kuner, H. (1999). *Fongers. Retrieved from* <www.rijwiel.net/fongersn.htm>.

Risseeuw, P. & Thurik, R. (2003). *Handboek ondernemers en adviseurs: management en economie van het midden- en kleinbedrijf*. Deventer: Kluwer.

Rogers, E.M. (1995). *Diffusion of innovations* (4th ed.) New York, NY: The Free Press.

Schumpeter, J. (1934). *The theory of economic development*. Cambridge, MA: Harvard University Press.

Shah, S. (2000). *Source and patterns of innovation in a consumers products field: Innovations in sporting equipment* (MIT Working Paper No. 4105).

Smith, W. (2008). *The history of the car seat*. Retrieved 31 October 2010 from <www.articlesbase.com/education-articles/the-history-of-the-car-seat-593547.html>..

Southworth, F.C. (1964). Family-tree diagrams. *Language*, **40**(4), 557–565.

Srivastava, L. (2005). Mobile phones and the evolution of social behaviour. *Behaviour & Information Technology, 24*(2), 111-129.

Steadman, P. (1979). *The evolution of designs: Biological analogy in architecture and the applied arts*. Cambridge, UK: Cambridge University Press.

Tanje, E. (2004). *Investeren in innovatie, Knelpunten en oplossingen voor het MKB*. The Hague: Kenniscentrum.

Tarn, J.N. (1973). *Five per cent philanthropy; An account of housing in urban areas between 1840 and 1914*. Cambridge, UK: Cambridge University Press.

Ten Klooster, R. (2002). *Packaging design, a methodological development and simulation of the design process*. Delft: Delft University of Technology.

Van Ammelrooy, P. (2005, November 4). Bellen is slechts bijzaak op de nieuwe gsm. *De Volkskrant, Bijlage Economie*.

Van den Hoed, R. (2004). *Driving fuel cell vehicles. How established industries react to radical technologies*. Delft: Design for Sustainability Program, Delft University of Technology.

Van der Wal, K. (2005). *Productfasen Fiets; Onderzoek & Ontwerp*. Unpublished master thesis, University of Twente, Enschede.

Van Eekelen, V.J.J.J. (2005). *Van Solex tot scooter; productfasen van de bromfiets*. Unpublished master thesis, University of Twente, Enschede.

Van Oost, E. (2003). Materialized gender: How shavers configure the users' femininity and masculinity. In N. Oudshoorn & T. Pinch (Eds.), *How users matter*. Cambridge, MA: The MIT Press.

Veblen, T. (1994). *The theory of the leisure class*. New York, NY: Penguin Books. (First published in 1899)

Woodring, C. (1987). Retailing new product or design. *Design Congress '87 Amsterdam*. Utrecht: Tekstotaal.

Yahoo Answers. (2011). *Beauty is in the eye of the beholder*. Retrieved 19 July 2011 from <answers.yahoo.com/question/index?qid=20071004192052AA CqS2G>.

Yang, X. (2001). *Economics: New classical versus neoclassical frameworks*. Malden, MA: Blackwell.

Ziman, J. (Ed.). (2000). *Technological innovation as an evolutionary process*. Cambridge, UK: Cambridge University Press..

## Figure Sources

| | |
|---|---|
| COVER | A-DNA B-DNA and Z-DNA, Richard Wheeler |
| FIGURE 2.1.1 | Motivaction International |
| FIGURE 2.3.1 | Crilly et al., 2004 |
| FIGURE 2.4.1 | Woodring, 1987 |
| FIGURE 4.1.1 | Ramakers, 1984 |
| FIGURE 4.1.2 | Ramakers, 1984 |
| FIGURE 4.1.3 | Van Oost, 2003 |
| FIGURE 4.1.4 | Van Oost, 2003 |
| FIGURE 4.1.5 | Van Oost, 2003 |
| FIGURE 4.1.7 | Philips Design |
| FIGURE 4.2.3 | International Telecommunication Union <www.itu.int> |
| FIGURE 4.2.8 | *Volkskrant Magazine*, 8 May 2004 |
| FIGURE 4.2.11 | Van Ammelrooy, 2005 |
| FIGURE 4.3.4 | www.moultonbicycles.co.uk |
| FIGURE 4.3.5 | www.bmxmuseum.com |
| FIGURE 4.3.6 | www.light-bikes.de |
| FIGURE 4.4.1 | Tarn, 1973 |
| FIGURE 4.4.2 | De Pauw, 2006 |
| FIGURE 4.4.3 | De Pauw, 2006 |
| FIGURE 4.4.6 | De Pauw, 2006 |
| FIGURE 4.5.1 | De Haan and Van der Vliet, 2005 |
| FIGURE 4.5.3 | De Haan and Van der Vliet, 2005 |
| FIGURE 4.5.4 | De Haan and Van der Vliet, 2005 |
| FIGURE 5.2.1 | Google Patents |
| FIGURE 5.2.2 | Google Patents |
| FIGURE 5.2.3 | Dorel, 2005 |
| FIGURE 5.2.4 | Dorel, 2005 and Consumentengids, 1970 |
| FIGURE 5.2.5 | Consumentengids, 1970 |
| FIGURE 5.2.6 | Google Patents |
| FIGURE 5.2.7 | Dorel, 2005 |
| FIGURE 5.2.9 | Consumentengids, 1993 |
| FIGURE 5.2.10 | Dorel, 2005 |
| FIGURE 7.3.10 | Eger et al., 2013 |

# ABOUT THE AUTHORS

## Prof. dr. ir. Arthur O. Eger

Arthur Eger (1950) studied Industrial Design Engineering at the Delft
University of Technology. In 1979 he was co-founder of the design
bureau Van Dijk/Eger/Associates (nowadays known as WeLL Design).
In 1996 he left the bureau to become the director of Space Expo, a space
museum and the official visitors centre of ESA, the European Space
Agency. In 2003 he became Professor at the University of Twente, Chair:
Product Design. Research area: Evolutionary Product Development.

Since 2004 he has been a member, and since 2009 the Chairman of the
Board, of the Department of Industrial Design Engineering of KIVI
NIRIA, the Royal Institution of Engineers in the Netherlands.

### Relevant Publications (Selection)

*Productontwerpen* (Product Design) (272 p.) (with Maarten Bonnema,
　　Eric Lutters en Mascha van der Voort (Lemma, The Hague, 1st print-
　　ing: 2004, 2nd printing: 2006, 3rd printing: 2008, 4th (completely
　　revised edition, 300 p.) printing: 2010)).

*Grafische Vormgeving voor Industrieel Ontwerpers* (subject: graphic
　　design) (190 p.) (Lemma, The Hague, 2010).

*Evolutionary Product Development* (two parts: 267 + 42 p.) (PhD thesis,
　　Delft University of Technology, Lemma, 2007).

*Van het eerste uur; Grondleggers van de Faculteit Industrieel Ontwerpen*
　　(subject: the History of the Faculty of Industrial Design Engineering
　　at the Delft University of Technology) (75 p.) (TU Delft, 2004).

*Create the Future*; Inaugural lecture, University of Twente (34 p.)
　　(September 2004, Enschede).

*Productontwikkeling en verpakkingsontwerp; checklisten marketing
　　management modellen* (subjects: product design and packaging
　　design) (Kluwer Bedrijfswetenschappen, Deventer, 1997; in 1998 these
　　checklists were published digital as well).

*Succesvolle Productontwikkeling* (Successful Product Development)
　　(135 p.) (Kluwer, 1996).

*Decoratieve Kunst* (Decorative Art) (160 p.) (Cantecleer, 1995).

*Digitaal Vormgeven* (subject: Desk Top Publishing) (144 p.) (Cantecleer,
　　1991).

**Editor**

*Vormgeven aan flexibele woonwensen* (subject: Architecture) (95 p.)
(Uitgeverij Delwel, The Hague, 1991).

*Linksaf, rechtsaf, alsmaar rechtdoor* (subject: Signposting) (170 p.)
(Catalogue with an exhibition, GVN, 1976).

*Stadsbewegwijzering* (subject: Signposting) (80 p.) (Proceedings of the
symposium, Studiecentrum Verkeerstechniek SVT, May 1978).

*Tekst in Beeld* (Dutch version of Michael Beaumont's *Type & Colour*)
(152 p.) (Cantecleer, 1988).

*De nieuwe doelgroep* (subject: Architecture) (30 p.) (Slokker, Huizen,
1990).

**Further Activities**

- Member of many juries, including: Aluminium Award, Good
Industrial Design Award, the Dutch Design Awards (Nederlandse
Designprijzen), Design for All Award, ESEF Engineering Award
(Chair), Shell LiveWIRE Young Business Award (Chair).
- Author of over 100 publications in both professional and scientific
journals.

## Ir. Huub Ehlhardt

Huub Ehlhardt (1971) studied Industrial Design Engineering at Delft
University of Technology (the Netherlands). Since 1995 he has worked
in the field of New Product Development, Cost and Value Engineering.
Currently the author is employed by Philips Electronics. Since 2010
he has combined his work in industry with a part-time PhD at the
University of Twente, where the focus of his research is on describing
technical innovation as an evolutionary process.

**Relevant Publications**

Ehlhardt, H. (2012). Child restraint systems: An analysis of their
development from an evolutionary perspective. *Journal of Design
Research*, **10**(4), 324-343.

Ehlhardt, H. & Tuinzaad, B. (2003). Kostenreductie door analyse
productontwerp en assemblageproces (Cost reduction by analyzing
product design and assembly process). *Product*, **11**(7), 28-31.

## Ir. Ferry Vermeulen

Ferry Vermeulen (1978) studied Industrial Design Engineering at Delft
University of Technology (the Netherlands). In 2006 he founded Fever,
an industrial design agency with a strong focus on industrial products.
To gain more knowledge in the field of successful product development,
he began his doctoral research in 2009. The focus of his research is on
developing low-risk innovation strategies to strengthen a company's
competitive position.

In 2010 the author founded a second company, named Manualise
(www.manualise.com). Manualise is a company specialized in manual

creation and services many well-known brands such as Halfords, Skil, Akai and Eneco.

**Relevant publications**

Vermeulen, F.G.A. (2012). Test 'm Zelf – Applicatie Productfasenmodel. *Product*, 20(2), 23-25.

Vermeulen, F.G.A. (2010). EPRO *innovation tool, a method for generating innovation strategies*. <www.designmanagementeurope.com>.

Vermeulen, F.G.A. (2009). Innoveren of Sterven. BNO *Vormberichten*, 6, 11.

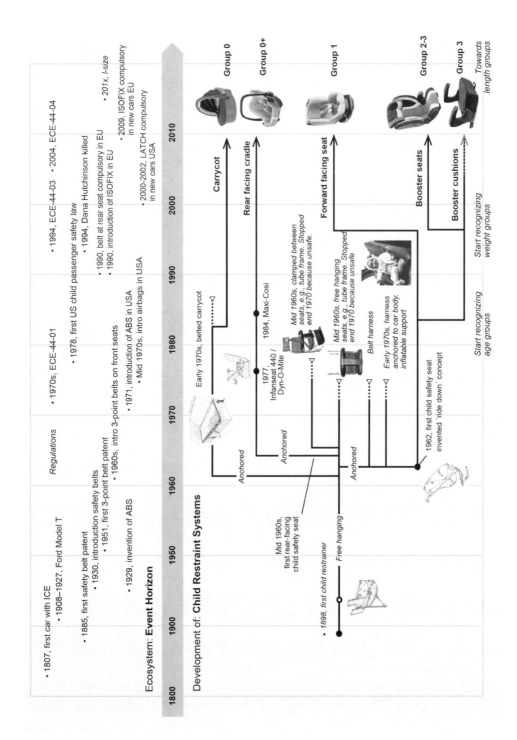

FIGURE 5.3.1
The product family tree of CRSS.

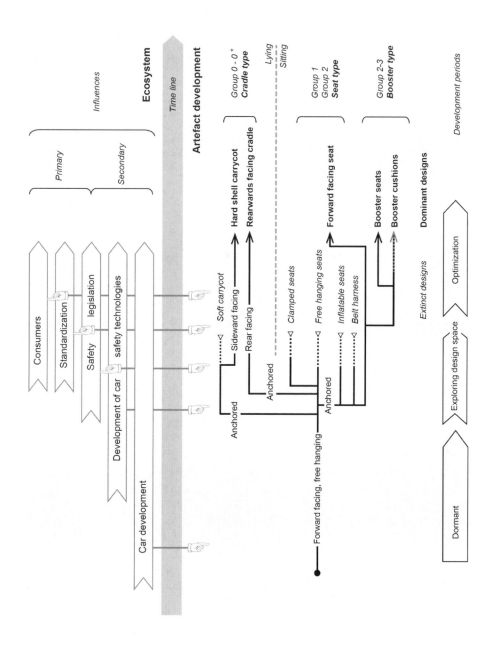

FIGURE 5.3.2
The relation between
artefact and ecosystem.

141